Reclaiming Lives from Sexual Violence

This book takes an innovative approach to using narrative therapy in counselling people who have been subject to childhood sexual abuse.

Reclaiming Lives from Sexual Violence presents an illustrative case study of the authors, Tim the therapist in consultation with Dale the client, who was sexually abused as a child by a clergy member. The book is unique in documenting their therapeutic work using transcripts taken directly from their sessions together. This narrative approach invites the reader to consider different ways of engaging in therapy in order to challenge the dominant social discourses around masculinity and shame.

Looking at shame from a position of value awareness rather than a deficit perspective, this book extends counselling to consider the individual experience as political and one that must be shared outside the one-to-one therapy environment. This will be an essential resource for beginning or established therapists and practitioners working with clients who have been victims of sexual violence.

Tim Donovan is a registered mental health social worker, an experienced practitioner passionate about assisting people in living their lives in their preferred way. With graduate qualifications in social work and narrative therapy, Tim is committed to person-centred practice in supporting individuals, families and groups who have experienced acts of oppression.

Dale Johns is a survivor of childhood sexual violence who has devoted his life to Pastoral Care and Advocacy, working with the lonely, homeless and drug affected. Dale hopes his story brings freedom to other survivors through gaining a deeper understanding of shame, and teaching mental health professionals showing care and compassion is a vital component of effective counselling.

Reclaiming Lives from Sexual Violence

Understanding Shame through Innovative Narrative Therapy

Tim Donovan and Dale Johns

LONDON AND NEW YORK

Cover image: © Orry Johns, 'Fight for Justice', 2021

First published 2022
by Routledge
4 Park Square, Milton Park, Abingdon, Oxon OX14 4RN

and by Routledge
605 Third Avenue, New York, NY 10158

Routledge is an imprint of the Taylor & Francis Group, an informa business

© 2022 Tim Donovan, Dale Johns

The right of Tim Donovan and Dale Johns to be identified as authors of this
work has been asserted in accordance with sections 77 and 78 of the Copyright,
Designs and Patents Act 1988.

All rights reserved. No part of this book may be reprinted or reproduced or
utilised in any form or by any electronic, mechanical, or other means, now
known or hereafter invented, including photocopying and recording, or in any
information storage or retrieval system, without permission in writing from the
publishers.

Trademark notice: Product or corporate names may be trademarks or registered
trademarks, and are used only for identification and explanation without intent to
infringe.

British Library Cataloguing-in-Publication Data
A catalogue record for this book is available from the British Library

Library of Congress Cataloging-in-Publication Data
Names: Donovan, Tim, author. | Johns, Dale, author.
Title: Reclaiming lives from sexual violence : understanding shame through
innovative narrative therapy / Tim Donovan, Dale Johns.
Description: Abingdon, Oxon ; New York, N.Y. : Routledge, 2022. | Includes
bibliographical references and index.
Identifiers: LCCN 2021046515 | ISBN 9781032188898 (paperback) | ISBN
9781032188928 (hardback) | ISBN 9781003256816 (ebook)
Subjects: MESH: Johns, Dale. | Child Abuse, Sexual--therapy | Adult Survivors
of Child Abuse--psychology | Narrative Therapy--methods | Shame | Adult |
Child | Personal Narrative
Classification: LCC HV6626.5 | NLM WM 167 | DDC 362.76--dc23
LC record available at https://lccn.loc.gov/2021046515

ISBN: 978-1-032-18892-8 (hbk)
ISBN: 978-1-032-18889-8 (pbk)
ISBN: 978-1-003-25681-6 (ebk)

DOI: 10.4324/9781003256816

Typeset in Bembo
by SPi Technologies India Pvt Ltd (Straive)

We would like to dedicate this book to our fathers, who showed vulnerability in sharing their own personal journeys with us, with emotion and sensitivity. They will never know how much this guided us to be the men we are today.

Contents

	Lists of illustrations	ix
	Foreword	x
	A personal testimony to Dale's story	xii
	Preface	xiv
	Acknowledgments	xvi
	Introduction	1
1	Paying reverence to the stories we hear	7
2	Ethics of care and understanding practices of self	10
3	Revealing and grasping the coat of shame	13
4	The politics of men's pain – informing our 'walking alongside' each other	18
5	Deconstructing negative identity conclusions	20
6	Exposing the coat of shame and fighting to claim what is already yours	29
7	Positioning yourself in ways that acknowledge strength in what you stand for	35
8	Wrestling through shame and sharing stories of resistance	54
9	Discerning shame and speaking the truth with integrity – Dale's Tree of Life	62

viii   *Contents*

10 Dale's re-claiming of integrity – '*sharing a glimpse of my story with explicit detail*'   71

11 The joining of stories as a political act   75

12 Making visible the signs of social and psychological resistance   81

13 Dale moving out into the world with confidence in knowing the truth and having a deeper understanding of shame   86

14 Connecting it all together – linking neurobiology, the body and narrative practice with Dale's emotions, through story telling   89

Reference   94
Appendix A   Therapeutic letter – Responding to trauma   97
Appendix B   Narrative Maps   98
Appendix C   Interview with 'Shame' practice questions   100
Appendix D   Interview with 'Integrity' practice questions   104
Appendix E   Re-membering Conversations practice map questions   108
Appendix F   Tree of Life project   110
Appendix G   Dale's Tree of Life   115
Appendix H   Signs of Social and Psychological Resistance   116
Index   118

Illustrations

Figures

6.1	Whiteboard notes describing Dale revealing the control of the perpetrator	34
9.1	Whiteboard notes of Dale describing lived experiences where he is not alone	70
G.1	Dale's adaptation of his Tree of Life	115

Tables

0.1	Overview of practice methods using a narrative therapy approach	3
6.1	Invitations to Integrity continuum using arrow	32
9.1	People of significance who have reminded Dale of the significance of him sharing the truth	67
11.1	The significance of creating space for two males to share the truth	76
12.1	Signs of social and psychological resistance	82

Foreword

Dale Johns and Tim Donovan approached me to write this foreword and I am deeply appreciative.

I first met Tim after he asked me to speak with him about his work as a school counsellor. I immediately experienced a flow of warmth, sensitivity and attentiveness, which made our conversations a joy. And although I briefly met Dale once before reading this book, I have got to know something of his dignified story through the bold and precious words that follow this foreword.

After reading their remarkable book my mind is alive with images and life-offering phrasing.

I think of Dale's reflection, 'I think for me, freedom is found in sharing the truth and its outcomes'. Such a sentiment reminds me of how remarkable an act of reclamation it is to even speak the horrors of child sexual abuse, and this book is a powerful expression of such speaking.

I reflect on Robert Miller's personal testimony, and his chilling comment, as he and Dale were to start their connection with St Mary's recreational boys' group, 'how could we have known the danger we were in?' In his testimony I bear witness to enduring friendship, and a shared hope for healing for those who have experienced childhood sexual abuse and trauma.

On every page I am greeted with knowledge that is born out of a gentle and persistent partnership between Dale and Tim, of walking alongside each other. Knowledge Dale contributed to Tim of giving voice to his preferred way to work. And where Tim contributed to Dale a space where he was believed, with no judgment, and where Dale was led in the direction of his truth as Tim worked gently, asking the right questions.

And on every page, I witness an intricate and delicate therapeutic approach being elaborated. This is an approach of respect and experimentation, accompanying great clarity in the use of narrative practices. It is accompanied by Tim's warm invitations for the reader to reflect on our own practice where we might find echoes of his deeply considered exploration. And where I am moved to use so many of the practices being articulated – perhaps starting with Tim's innovation in using David Denborough's signs of social and psychological resistance in working with trauma and abuse.

I am also greeted with images of some of the more recent history of the heartbreaking and beautiful work within these pages. While reading this book my mind was cast back to my days as a young social worker in the early to mid 1990s. I was co-facilitating groups for male survivors of sexual assault, along with a co-facilitator who was a survivor of sexual violence. I was so very uncertain about how to do this work. I think of how feminist scholarship, activism and therapy, and books such as *The Courage to Heal Workbook* by Laura Davis, *Discoveries* by Sheridan Linnell and Dorothy Cora and *Father Daughter Rape* by Biff Ward, offered us a path. This work and such books gifted us language, concepts, and a program to start to respond meaningfully to men who had been sexually abused, a response that was so very desperately overdue. Alongside these supporting histories for *Reclaiming Lives from Sexual Violence*, I found myself imagining my powerful appreciation and frankly, relief, if this book were available for others and me as we set off trying to find meaningful therapeutic responses to sexual violence towards men all those years ago.

There are two more images that I wish to share. This first is an image of an act of justice doing; of a story and a book going out into the world and making a powerful difference to our field and for those who have been subjected to sexual violence. This is indeed a story, a life lived so far that has not been for nothing but is making a powerful reclamation.

There is one more image I have. I am thinking of the words Dale imagined his father would share if he could comment on his journey, 'dad would be sobbing . . . joy in knowing what he had achieved through what I shared, and hurt in realising how hard it all was'.

I find myself joining with Dale's father's sentiment. However, I would add that I see more joy than hurt being cultivated as a result of this book going out into the word. I know this book will offer companionship and ideas for workers who also, perhaps like me, desperately wish to offer a meaningful response to sexual violence. And it will offer sustenance and comradery for others who know something of the hurt and joy of their journeys in reclaiming their lives from sexual violence.

David Newman (Director of Sydney Narrative Therapy and Faculty member of The Dulwich Centre)

A personal testimony to Dale's story

Dale Johns is my friend now, and has been for fifty-eight years. We grew up together in the Central Victorian town of Inglewood, surrounded by grand old buildings, a proud legacy of the 1860s gold rush, and the economic boom and bust of the 1880s that followed. Our forebears were the original seekers, convicts, miners, farmers, shopkeepers; they took their chances and helped to establish a community. Amongst the architectural gems stand four fine churches, the largest and the most impressive being the Catholic Church of St Mary's, which is perfectly perched on a hill looking out across the town. In the mid-1960s, we were enrolled together in the local state school; we served at the altar of St Augustine's Church of England; we played alongside each other in the sporting and community clubs; and our families were closely connected through local history and traditions. In the summer of 1973–74, Dale and I walked to the top of the hill, following an invitation to visit St Mary's recreational boys' group. It was our introduction to its overseer and priest Father Gerald Ridsdale. How could we have known the danger we were in . . . .

In the years that followed, Dale and I were violently sexually abused hundreds of times by Father Ridsdale. It is now known through Ridsdale's televised testimony at the Royal Commission, is his accepted acknowledgment of the truth that his abusing of boys in Inglewood, at that time was out of control. His insistence that the abuse was in fact a shared physical love that had a sacred purpose, wasn't for us to question, but for us to uphold – for God's will was holy. In light of all this our secret would remain upheld for the next forty years. In April 2014 the shocking revelations contained in our separate charge lists were read out in the County Court in Melbourne in our presence, and seated at the rear of the court was Gerald Ridsdale, disconnected and head bowed. A shocking moment of realisation, that Ridsdale's frivolous religious language had successfully silenced us was astonishing.

Dale has gone on to greater things – he has co-authored this book with his counsellor and mentor, Tim Donovan. Their collaborative presentations across Australia have elevated Narrative Therapy as a vital and humane contribution to the mental health sector. *Reclaiming Lives from Sexual Violence* is an invaluable gift of truth and resilience, and a stunning journey of triumph, generously shared to the world.

It is a truly remarkable achievement of seven years of dedicated work, and an important acknowledgment of the vital worth of Narrative Therapy. This is a book for all of us to reflect upon, and to benefit from. Through gentle conversation and a shared trust, they were able to gradually unlock the burden of Dale's lifelong

A personal testimony to Dale's story xiii

secret of violent sexual abuse, exposing the torturous years of hidden shame. Dale's fearless honesty and enduring courage to share his story was inspired through Tim's perceptive guidance, and together they confronted shame. With an imaginative exchange of narrative, they succeeded in expunging little by little the years of torment, emerging with new-found freedoms and the reassurance of an acquired wisdom to carry Dale forward.

It is my hope that all victims of abuse and trauma will find peace out of pain.

Robert Miller

Preface

A unique feature of this book, *Reclaiming Lives from Sexual Violence*, is that Dale – who was sexually abused as a child by a clergy member at the local Catholic Church – is centred in the narrative. The focus is on Dale as the expert in forming and reclaiming his life. By not imposing my own agenda in our therapeutic work, Dale was able to give further context to his experiences of sexual violence. Thus, during our many conversations, Dale's skills, abilities and hard-won knowledge were made visible; furthermore, Dale gave me hope for the other people I consulted with.

So you can appreciate the significance of our story and what is represented in this book, I offer some background for context. In the early stages of practising as a social worker, my enthusiasm was led by a desire to contribute deeper meaning to people's lives. My ideals incorporated concepts of social justice and 'finding voice' for the individuals, families and groups I walked alongside. What you are about to embark on is a walk down this path, witnessing first-hand the therapeutic journey Dale and I took together over approximately three and a half years.

As I explored therapeutic models that fitted with my life philosophy, and which I could easily understand, I was challenged with feelings of uncertainty and vulnerability regarding the knowledge and skills I brought to the profession. I was not overly familiar with therapeutic interventions such as cognitive behavioural therapy (CBT), psychodynamic theory and schema therapy – and these models were often talked about and emphasised as a 'magic potion'. So during my early days as a social worker, the feeling of being under-equipped and under the microscope from peers resonated strongly. To counter this, I found cultivating 'practices of self' into my work useful, emphasising my values, principles and techniques of transparency, accountability, working collaboratively and paying reverence to clients' sharing of stories.

Over time, I became primarily focused on counselling in my practice, and by the time I met Dale, I was working for a specialised service counselling survivors of sexual abuse. During this time, I felt confronted by the language used by my colleagues when they were talking about a client's experiences of abuse. The focus was often on conveying only one story of identity, and that was not representative of my experience with the multiple stories a client generally presents with. Similarly, I was particularly challenged by the use of models of therapeutic practice that focused on the problems of the person. Furthermore, I felt pressured to align with these ideas that diagnosed and treated the problem. In contrast, what interested me was exploring the client's 'acts of resistance' to the problems they faced and how their experiences of sexual abuse compromised their values, which often silenced them from living life in their preferred way. This will be expanded upon further, later in the book.

During this time, I came across a therapy that seemed to align with how I wished to position my counselling practice. Known as 'narrative therapy', in this model of practice the therapist is decentred as the expert and influential in the conversation (White 2007, p. 39).

My walk (journey) with Dale became instrumental in the development of my narrative therapy practice and further tertiary studies – so much so, Dale gave me the opportunity to give voice to how I preferred to work. As a result, narrative therapy has now become my dominant model of practice. Michael White, considered to be the founder of narrative therapy, highlights that – in the context of therapeutic work – it is often only the problem stories in people's lives that we hear and pay attention to. This book, *Reclaiming Lives from Sexual Violence,* highlights an ethical way of working, assuming that people who consult with us have meaning-making skills developed over their lives and that people are always telling stories and giving meaning to these experiences (White 2007).

Finally, dominant therapeutic discourses are in danger of positioning the health practitioner or counsellor as the expert. This power dynamic can play into a client potentially walking away from a consultation with self-doubt and unrealistic expectations about their road to recovery. Often, clients question their own ability to get through tough times, and therefore feel the need to continue engaging in therapy in order to feel well again. This over-reliance can be hazardous and potentially keep the person in a space of not moving beyond the victim story. In this book, Dale and I give significant consideration to challenging these ideas around expert-driven therapy. As Michael White (2011, p. 31) eloquently writes about the importance of self-reflection in our therapeutic work:

It is because I love my work that I am highly motivated to identify any abuses of power and to root them out. I believe that if one is not tripping across abuses of power in one's therapeutic practice, it means one has gone to sleep.

What are your intentions when engaging in therapeutic conversations? Do you provide the space to reflect on your work – by yourself or with others? Do you find ways to advocate for your own way of practice, if your preferred models of therapy are not fully supported in the organisation you work for?

Finally, I will leave you with a quote from Michel Foucault (1995) to reflect upon as you read through this book – maybe you already position yourself in this way? I hope you are inspired to be vulnerable and innovative in your own work.

He who is subjected to a field of visibility, and who knows it, assumes responsibility for the constraints of power; he makes them play spontaneously upon himself; he inscribes in himself the power relation in which he simultaneously plays both roles; he becomes the principle of his own subjection.

Through sharing Dale's story, I hope that it will get you thinking about what is possible in your own practice – what you place importance on and what motivates you in your practice.

Tim Donovan

Acknowledgments

From Tim Donovan

I would like to acknowledge, in no particular order, the following people for their contributions to this book. They have provided me with humour, robust conversations, and warmth in supporting my many ideas and enthusiasm. To my dad, Bob Donovan, who was always open to hearing about my ideas, for his support in getting me motivated to believe in myself when it counted. To my mum, Louise Donovan, for always being up for the conversation when challenging me on my normalised judgements and pushing me to challenge the status quo. To Carolyn Donovan, my life-long partner, wife and friend and narrative practitioner by proxy. To Dale Johns, my colleague and friend, and the inspiration to keep me working in this area and remaining vulnerable. To Stephen Whittle, mentor and friend who believed in me and encouraged me to take risks. To Tarn Kaldor, colleague and friend who provided the feedback I needed to hear and was able to ask the questions that got me thinking. To Ron Findlay, who inspired me to delve deeply when reflecting on my own intentions behind the questions I asked in therapy and impressed to me the importance of having sound knowledge of the philosophical underpinnings of narrative therapy. To David Denborough, for his graciousness and willingness to engage in my project thesis with rigour, which is now being published. To Sue Davidson, mentor, friend and previous work colleague, who enabled me to be vulnerable and encouraged me to think beyond the problem story. To Marti Block, mentor and friend, who supported me in many ways and continues to do so. To David Newman, supervisor and mentor who provided clarity in my thinking and ideas. To Heather Millar, for her attention to detail in editing the text of our book. Also, the conversations I have had and continue to have with family, friends, peers, and work colleagues continue to motivate and inspire me. Above all, to the many people I have consulted with who have taught me how to listen with greater intent and reflect on my own self-practice – I wouldn't have gotten to this point without you. Thank you for the hard-won knowledge I have gained from those interactions where you assumed a position of powerlessness upon first entering the therapeutic space. I hope that I have in some part enabled you to speak with greater authority, challenging the power structures that come within the walls of the clinical setting of therapy.

Acknowledgments   xvii

From Dale Johns

I would like to acknowledge the following people who have given me the strength to break my silence and to release my story and very personal notes. Firstly, to my Lord and Saviour Jesus for his constant presence – I live today because of His love. Thank you again to Tim Donovan, counsellor, colleague and friend, for his amazingly caring work ethic and his incredible support 'walking alongside' me and bringing me to this place today of working together and co-authoring this book. To my late father Albert Johns, for his love and advice and for being a fine example for me to aspire to, and for providing and teaching me great Christian values. To my mum Valerie Johns – for being an amazing mum, believing in me and for your constant love, example, advice and support. To my darling wife Caroline – for always trusting me, for your unflinching love and for staying by my side through it all – the years of me being dreadfully depressed, the nightmares and interrupted sleep, and all the other idiosyncrasies. To my darling children Orry, Lakarra, and Tayo, for loving me unconditionally, even when my overprotectiveness was smothering, and for your trust, strength and support. My siblings Karen, Trevor and Tim for your faith, prayer and trust in me. To Robert, my constant life-long friend – for sharing each other's pain, the thousands of hours of supportive chats and believing in each other. To my friends Jane and Robyn and Jen, who have supported me in so many ways, and who loved, prayed and cared for me when I felt so unworthy. Thank you all for carrying me when I couldn't carry myself and lifting me up in prayer, your constancy has been amazing. Love you all.

Introduction

There are many pervasive myths surrounding childhood sexual violence, which can influence the way people who have experienced it view themselves – for example, 'men and boys should be able to defend themselves' and 'men cannot and should not share their feelings openly'. These myths give context to my walk with Dale – specifically, how these polarising judgements can fuel shame and silence a person from sharing the truth of their experience. Together, Dale and I were able to openly challenge these myths, which informed our future work and enabled the creation of this book. The social acceptance of these myths not only silences people who have experienced sexual violence, it obscures the *reality* of the abuse. Thus, by confronting these myths, we can create an opening for a survivor to resist the silencing effects of shame, to gain distance from a problem-saturated life story, and to identify values and commitments that can provide a basis for a meaningful life that is not defined by the experience of abuse.

Reclaiming lives from sexual violence demonstrates the application of narrative practice to counselling people who have been subject to childhood sexual violence (White 2007; Epston and White 1990). Narrative practice provides useful strategies for deconstructing unhelpful cultural discourses or myths; for identifying and strengthening the skills and knowledge people have regarding their own problems; and for encouraging people's connection with preferred ways of being. These ideas may be appropriate to others seeking respectful and non-pathologising ways of working with children, adolescents and adults who have experienced ongoing effects from childhood sexual abuse.

At the time Dale presented for counselling he had been silent for forty-two years. He was troubled by memories associated with his experiences of sexual violence. He felt that these experiences had come to define him, leaving him unsure about who he was. In keeping with narrative principles, Dale's experiences, preferences and understandings were placed at the centre of counselling (Morgan and White 2006, p. 71). I did not offer advice, evaluation or professional opinions; instead, Dale was invited to 'become the primary author' of his own story (Morgan 2000, p. 96). I was influential not by imposing solutions, but by offering a scaffolding of questions to support the development of Dale's own thinking. This involved listening for moments of discomfort and experiences that had been obscured by the influence of shame. Over time, these practices enabled Dale to move away from shame and uncertainty, and towards a life lived according to his own values. With a

DOI: 10.4324/9781003256816-1

2 Introduction

deeper understanding of shame, Dale was able to share his experience to help others who had been through similar experiences.

Early on, to emphasise the importance of naming our therapeutic alliance and how we engaged in conversation, Dale and I came up with the 'walking alongside' metaphor to describe our approach to the space we were sharing. I continue to use this metaphor in my practice today and I thank Dale for that.

Here are some questions you could consider in your own work setting to explore this analogy of 'shared space':

- We try *not* to be ahead of someone, so how do we catch ourselves when we are?
- Are we alongside them always?
- When might we step ahead and is that ever a good idea?
- How can we use the analogy of 'space' when looking at how we move ahead in the terrain?
- Is there another form of transport that would be more useful than 'walking alongside'?
- What terrain are we on – is it a climb, on even ground, up and down?
- Over time, is the terrain changing?

What made the description of 'walking alongside' useful for Dale? Was it that Dale preferred me in a particular instance to be beside him, half a step behind, or ahead, to venture with? In Dale's own words from 2018:

> It was extremely important, this metaphor 'walking alongside', because it put me in the centre of the conversation and my situation while you supported me. You actually led the conversation asking the right questions, while 'walking alongside' me. Because I had that solid support and was asked the right questions, which opened the way for me to deal with shame and guilt, enabling me to break the silence that I had held for forty-two years.

In this book, Dale and I will walk you through our therapeutic journey, which spanned more than three and a half years. Using transcripts taken directly from our sessions, you will learn ways to carry conversations using narrative therapy approaches. The intention of using transcripts in this way is to illustrate how narrative therapy can contribute to the therapeutic process and how you can use it in your own context when consulting with others. Therefore, these conversations are to be used as a guide, and I would encourage you to be innovative in adapting your own questions specific to your own practice setting.

Drawing on the work of Michael White (1997, 2007), Alan Jenkins (1998, 2007) and David Denborough (2008), some of the particular themes we explored include the 'politics of men's pain', 'ethics of care', 'position of the practitioner', and 'sharing of stories representing a political act'. In addition, we incorporated specific narrative therapy maps including 'externalising conversations', 're-authoring conversations', 're-membering' conversations and the Tree of Life activity. The maps assisted Dale and I to better understand the effects associated with a person's experiences of sexual violence, in particular Dale's shame. Included in the appendices are examples of narrative therapy methods used that may give you some ideas to use in your own practice, including a therapeutic letter, interviewing the problem, re-membering conversation questions used with Dale, and an example of Dale's Tree of Life in completion.

Throughout the book, I also refer to other people's words and experiences shared in therapeutic sessions; for ethical reasons pseudonyms have been used. These conversations are presented in **bolded italic text**. Though there is a focus on Dale's experiences of sexual violence, other stories have been weaved within Dale's narrative to highlight that the method adopted with Dale has benefited many others as well – including children, adolescents and adults, without gender bias. Finally, the reader is taken to a place where Dale's experience of sexual violence represents a political act. Dale is able to share his story with a deeper understanding of shame and to positively contribute to other people who have experienced sexual violence. Furthermore, Dale's ideas around therapy are able to be shared with professionals who work in the field of care and support.

Ultimately, this book demonstrates how narrative therapy approaches can be applied in counselling people who have been subject to sexual violence, and it is hoped these methods can also be used in other therapeutic and support contexts. You will learn practical ways to use narrative therapy in deconstructing unhelpful dominating societal discourses and myths around sexual violence; in identifying and strengthening the skills and knowledge people have regarding their own problems; and in encouraging connection with people's preferred ways of being.

When mapping our journey, Table 0.1 represents an overview of the main themes presented and how narrative therapy ideas have contributed. Influence has been drawn from White's *Re-authoring lives: Interviews and Essays* (1995). Refer to Appendix B for an overview of other narrative maps used and referred to in the book.

Table 0.1 Overview of practice methods using a narrative therapy approach

PRACTICE	APPROACH	EFFECT
The position of the therapist/counsellor / practitioner	– Decentred and influential – Double listening for the absent but implicit in conversations – Being mindful of the position of power within the practitioner–client relationship	– Open curiosity with a sense of wonder associated with the questions – Relationship building – Collaborative effort in trying to understand why the client is consulting the practitioner – Transparency, i.e. sharing of case notes, including using a white board – Using the client's words and not the practitioner reframing and interpreting the words said

4   *Introduction*

PRACTICE	APPROACH	EFFECT
Uncovering the coat of shame	- Externalising conversations - Statement of Position of the client regarding the problem story and identifying the thin traces of the alternate stories that are starting to appear - Exploring the client's 'acts of resistance' from their experiences of sexual violence - Paying attention to what is 'absent but implicit' when listening for the client's values and beliefs	- Exploring 'what the shame is about' while acknowledging the person's experiences of sexual violence and its effects on them and others close to them - Supporting the client to explore what they value in life and their beliefs of the world - Supporting the client to come to a new identity construction through an acceptance or reconnection to their own values and beliefs
Deconstructing negative identity conclusions	- Re-authoring unique outcomes and responses to the client's experiences of sexual violence - Reclaiming the client's values and beliefs - Re-membering conversations to thicken up the client's new identity conclusions	- Thickening up of the client's values and beliefs through the sharing of past, present and future events - Thickening up of the client's new identity construction - Attempting to separate the differences between the perpetrator and the client - Recognising that the abuse is not the client's fault

PRACTICE	APPROACH	EFFECT
Taking off the coat of shame and reclaiming what was yours	– Moving the client from the feelings of shame to taking responsibility for their own values and beliefs through re-authoring conversations and re-membering conversations – Exploring 'rites of passage' with the client regarding their growth in reclaiming their values and beliefs – Collective narrative practice initiatives – for instance, responding to the social issues of sexual violence through letter writing to other sexual abuse survivors – Tree of Life – places in context the problem story, i.e. understanding the negative effects of shame, which can now be identified as a thin description of the person's identity	– Sharing the experiences of the new identity construction in context to past, present and future events – Creating a collective understanding of the client's experiences in context to the person's life stories using the metaphor of a tree – Developing the richness of the client's life, where the dominant story is now their new positive identity construction – Gaining a deeper understanding of shame, and trying to pay reverence to what the person values and believes – Storying signs of social and psychological resistance, through the client's lived experiences – Joining in a collective endeavour in addressing the social issue through the client's local knowledge from what they experienced

6   *Introduction*

PRACTICE	APPROACH	EFFECT
The joining of stories as a political act	- Joining in a collective endeavour in addressing the social issue of sexual violence through the sharing of the client's local knowledge from what they experienced - Putting context to the 'problem story' – understanding the negative effects of shame, which can now be viewed as an indication of a client's value awareness	- Challenging dominant discourses surrounding sexual assault counselling that needs to be individual, where stories cannot be shared for fear of the person not being able to relive these experiences in a public setting - The individual experiences of sexual violence becoming a community initiative to 'stop the silence ... stop the sexual abuse' - Sharing of skills and knowledges of self that are resisting the negative effects of the sexual violence - Bringing forth value awareness and having the last say on issues of personal identity
Moving out into the world with confidence in knowing the truth and having a deeper understanding of shame	- The client having the say on when the therapeutic journey should come to a close - Opening of space for the client to perform preferred stories of their lives	- Contributing to other people's lives and their preferred ways of being - An acknowledgment by the person of many of the alternative claims associated with these performances - The client discharging themselves from therapy

Dale and I are now embarking on sharing our therapeutic alliance with other practitioners through the 'Reclaiming lives from sexual violence' workshop. This book, *Reclaiming lives from sexual violence*, is a resource for you to use with the workshop and in your own practice.

1 Paying reverence to the stories we hear

Key points to consider

- <u>Double listening</u>: *Listening for accounts of how people have responded to their trauma.*
  - *Listening for the stories of self that lay beyond the problem story.*
- <u>Self-awareness in your practice</u>: *Knowing when you are pushing your own agenda.*
  - *Seeing the client as the expert in their own lived experiences.*

A narrative worldview supports the belief that no matter how compelling any given story might be, no matter how powerfully it is entrenched, there are always other stories. Michael White (2003) names the ability to hear both stories as 'double listening'. Therefore, initially when the practitioner is listening to a person presenting problem stories of their suffering, their fears, their experience of sexual violence, at the same time, they can be listening for openings into stories that speak of other possibilities, alternative accounts of how people have responded to the trauma. Paying attention and drawing out the actions they may have taken during their experience of oppression requires continual reassurance and sensitivity from the practitioner. It depends on many factors as to when these conversations can be had – for instance, the person needs to be ready to move beyond the problem story. This can take time and requires patience from the practitioner. Exploring these reclaimed ideas of self can occur when the conversation moves towards the often-neglected stories of a person's response to their experience of sexual violence, and it can enable the excavation of what the person stands for and how they wish to live their life. Through conversations where the knowledge and experience of a person become more richly described, the person can identify with their own experiences. Furthermore, White (2003) used the term 'absent but implicit' to convey the understanding that in the expression of any experience of life, there is a discernment we make between the expressed experience and other experiences that have already been given meaning and provide a contrasting backdrop, thus shaping the expression being given attention to. In therapeutic conversations, we can use the concept of the 'absent but implicit' to enquire into the stories of self that lay beyond the problem story. For instance, a person's ability to discern their own despair implies that they also have hopes, dreams or visions that have been lost or weakened. Making visible the client's own positive identity conclusions has an intention for the client to reclaim what was already theirs.

DOI: 10.4324/9781003256816-2

8 *Paying reverence to the stories*

Early on with Dale, it was particularly important not to focus only on the negative impacts of the sexual abuse and the actions of the person that carried out the sexual abuse, though these conversations did occur, and at times in great detail over a number of sessions, as it was crucial to acknowledge the problem stories experienced by Dale. These stories were also important to acknowledge as they enabled Dale to feel heard and be clear on where he stood, indicating the actions of the person who carried out the sexual violence were morally wrong and physically abusive. Yet, our conversations also explored actions Dale took to place himself in a situation of safety during his experiences of sexual violence. These conversations drew upon an assumption that Dale's ability to withstand, get away from, disassociate from the pain and suffering experienced during the sexual violence placed him in a position of power, even if subtly, enabling Dale to take a position on his preferred identity. To illustrate this point, I have included an excerpt from a conversation I had with Mathew, a child I previously 'walked alongside'. Mathew was enabled to speak with conviction and freedom through his sharing of how he took action in resisting the sexual abuse. Finding openings where the practitioner can be curious, exploring exceptions to, or a time where, the person was not under the influence of the problem and was able to take a stand, however small, against the problem is a key tenet of narrative therapy. Angel Yuen (2007) named this as exploring the person's 'acts of resistance' to the oppressive influence of the problem. Acts of resistance are not only physical acts but can include thoughts that may contradict the way the problem would be causing the person to think. In particular, narrative therapy is about asking questions that enable the person to identify the alternative stories to the problem story (of abuse). For instance:

TIM: *What did you do to get yourself through what happened, to get yourself out of the situation* [… of being sexually abused]?

MATHEW: [Using the whiteboard, Mathew wrote a list of actions he took that enabled him to get himself out of the situation of being sexually abused.] *I used to say to the* 'bad fruit' *that I am tired and that I needed to go home, or sometimes I would say that I needed to call my brother.*

TIM: *What would you name this as… the ability to be able to say this to the* 'bad apple'?

MATHEW: *I would call it* 'courage'.

In future sessions, Mathew and I built upon these actions of 'courage' and examined how he had used this ability in past and present situations within other life contexts, and not only within his experiences of the abuse. The process of people re-authoring their lives involves noticing the 'quiet', unnoticed stories that are able to support them in 'reclaiming self' as they separate themselves from their problems. As Michael White wrote, these 'quiet' stories are often referred to in narrative practice as 'unique outcomes' or 'exceptions'. Effective therapy is about engaging people in the re-authoring of the compelling plights of their lives in ways that arouse curiosity about human possibility and in ways that invoke the play of imaginations (White 2007). Following on from my conversations with Mathew, their experiences were documented in the form of a therapeutic letter named as 'Mathew's actions of Life/Bravery' (refer to Appendix A). As a result, Mathew wasn't experiencing the distancing effects of therapy, where the expert analysis of the problem stems from the therapist and can potentially further silence the client from speaking out about their experiences for fear of self-doubt, shame and judgement.

Having the answers to the client's problems is not always possible. When I was initially consulting with Dale, my desire to grow his understanding of his experiences of shame was provoked. I would do this via particular questions, such as, how can someone who has experienced sexual violence take on the acts of the perpetrator when it wasn't their choice? At the time I was new to working in sexual assault, and I felt personally vulnerable due to the uncertainty I had around not being able to *fix* Dale's pain. Instead, I listened to Dale's expertise, relying upon his lived experiences. By exposing my vulnerability and asking Dale questions with curiosity and wonder, I was not relying on evidence-based theories. This was a reflection of my own questioning around dominant therapeutic models.

We all have knowledge, skills and experience we bring into our work setting that gives us certain competencies, enabling us to contribute to people's lives in significant ways. Therefore, how can we as professionals challenge dominant ideas of expert-driven service and become aware when we are pushing our own agenda in the therapeutic setting? Maybe you are already doing this? How were Dale and I able to challenge society's view of shame, particularly as to how sexual violence informs the client's view of themselves? I hope that this book honours the stories of the people I have 'walked alongside' – it is particularly important to distance myself from being the primary author of what has been written.

2 Ethics of care and understanding practices of self

Key points to consider

- <u>Consulting respectfully with the client</u>: *Being aware of your position of power and establishing safety in how you consult.*
- <u>Establishing safety in your consultation</u>: *Providing an environment for sensitive and vigilant conversations.*

Acknowledging a client's response to their experience of trauma, while listening with reverence to the often-intimate details of their lives, requires care and meticulous attention as they share their story. How do we do what we do respectfully when consulting with people? Working collaboratively and being transparent, while being aware of our position of power, requires continual self-analysis. Michael White (2000, p. 129) writes about the 'the belief that we need to be reclaiming these sorts of terms in the interpretation of what we are doing' in the therapeutic space. Without underestimating or under-acknowledging the influence of professional development, other work colleagues and professionals on one's practice, techniques of self-awareness and developing conscious knowledge of one's own character, feelings, motives, and desires can also profoundly impact the therapeutic interactions we have with a client. Furthermore, means of building relationships enhance conversations and our therapeutic alliance, which render possible the acknowledgement of the client in different ways that are not centred purely on the abuse. Michael White (2000, p. 150) writes about honouring these principles:

- Accountability: that is available in partnership with other people, opening up possibilities for us to become other than who we are on account of the conversations we have. For example, being genuine and open with other agencies, work colleagues and the people we see. And approaching conversations with a willingness to learn from others.
- Transparency: committing to the deconstruction of our own actions and the taken-for-granted ways of being in this work and thinking about life. For example, sharing case notes with the client, using the whiteboard in sessions and sharing this with the person as a record for them to keep hold of.

DOI: 10.4324/9781003256816-3

Ethics of care and understanding 11

- Working collaboratively: taking steps to prepare for new foundations for possibilities in the time it takes, and not being goal orientated. For example, involving the client in whiteboard conversations during the sessions, checking in with the client, and actively seeking feedback from the client.
- Developing an attitude of reverence: for the client's sharing of stories of their daily existence. For example, listening to the client's history of experiences and the meaning making they give to these hard-won knowledges. Writing down the client's words using their language when describing these experiences.
- Challenging the dominant beliefs and assumptions of our culture: for example, bringing into the sessions conversations that deconstruct society's beliefs and assumptions and how these inform the client's view of themselves and the view of yourself as the therapist.

Therefore, setting the scene when commencing a session for the first time is crucial if your intention is to promote an ongoing, open relationship of trust. Here are a couple of ways that I have chosen to commence a conversation with a client.

TIM: *Are you okay if I take notes and share them with you throughout the session, so that I am getting your words down correctly? And please let me know if I have misheard or written down something incorrectly. These are your notes and your experiences, which you can have at the end of our sessions.* [I then place an open paper book on a table, in the middle of the room, and/or use the whiteboard to document our conversation.]

TIM: *I will write down your words as I am interested and curious to hear about your experiences, as you are the expert in your own lived experiences. I am here to walk alongside you and the sessions could go in any direction – depending on the conversations that present. Are you okay with that, please let me know?*

It is generally held that having a framework for a session is important, because then there is structure and a consistency in how the sessions are conducted. However, arguably an open relationship and the process of asking questions, making discoveries, and testing those discoveries in the search for new understanding are equally important, if not more so, than the content of the counselling sessions (Erskine 1997 p. 22). Alan Jenkins (2009) stressed the importance of the practitioner's opening remarks, observations and responses in the initial conversations, in establishing this safe environment and thereby setting the tone for the whole session. Without this relationship it is difficult to create the safe, trusting environment that is necessary for effective therapeutic interventions.

Most of the people that mental health practitioners consult with in their work have experienced disadvantage or injustice in their lives, and the way we proceed initially can set the scene for a safe, therapeutic environment. By creating an environment for sensitive and vigilant conversations, we can promote agency and integrity for the client (Jenkins 2009). In being ready to listen and to challenge a client's feelings of shame, we may better understand the client's concerns. This type of inquiry requires genuine interest in the client's personal experiences – how they

12 *Ethics of care and understanding*

construct meaning for themselves and the perception of how they are viewed by others (Erskine 1997). By staying curious in your initial enquiries and responses, you remain accountable to your own practice as well as promoting a level of transparency and encouraging the client to speak more openly (Jenkins 2009). Not paying sufficient attention at this early stage could close down all conversation. The benefit of creating a safe space that encourages openness in conversation was reinforced early on in my 'walking alongside' Dale, through feedback I received after one of our sessions in 2015:

> I commit to the truth with integrity, where the deepest, most personal, private, difficult stuff I share, is heard, you hear it, stuff I have not uttered to anyone else, not even spoken loudly to myself and I don't feel judged, I think for me, freedom is found in sharing the truth and its outcomes in a space (which you create) for me … and I think that's really important not just for me but for anyone being counselled … to be in a similar space.

3 Revealing and grasping the coat of shame

Key points to consider:

- <u>Developing an understanding of the problem</u>: *Exploring shame as an indication of value awareness. Establishing alternate identity conclusions of self.*
- <u>Introduction to externalising conversations</u>: *Deconstructing the client's ideas of the problem and how they are informed.*
    - *The client establishing the courses of action available to them in attempting to lessen the effects of the problem on their lives.*

The origin of the word 'shame' is thought to derive from an older word meaning 'to cover', and as such, covering oneself, literally or figuratively, is a natural expression of shame (Lewis 1971). It is important as a practitioner to understand the notion of shame in a more broad sense, if we are to appreciate the meaning that a client presenting for counselling has of shame, founded on their own history, culture, values and beliefs. This will influence the person's identity construction, shaped from their experiences of sexual violence.

As identified by Michael Lewis (1992) in his book *Shame: the exposed self,* shame is a negative, painful, social emotion that results from comparison of the self's action with the self's standards. Shame burns at the core of our human condition, which arguably is central to the biblical story of Adam and Eve in Western culture, and it also functions as a powerful deterrent to socially unacceptable behaviour.

Yet what causes us shame is specific to culture and era, according to Northwestern University historian Deborah Cohen (2013). The Secretariat of National Aboriginal and Islander Child Care (SNAICC) (2014) defined shame as the response a child has to 'personal failure or inadequacy', which in an Aboriginal or Torres Strait Islander context can result from the 'deep-seated feelings of shame and low self-esteem' that many Aboriginal and Torres Strait Islander people experience as part of the pervasive legacy of colonisation and dispossession. Shame can influence people to be reluctant to speak or take action in front of others, or be seen to be standing out too much – the effects being that a person begins to question what they have done wrong. Barbara Wingard (2011) in her article 'Bringing lost loved ones into our conversations: Talking about loss in honouring ways', writes about the importance of people knowing:

DOI: 10.4324/9781003256816-4

14   *Revealing and grasping the coat*

They can talk about losses in ways that don't bring more pain because, if you think talking about it is going to focus on the pain, this can create more silence. People may choose not to talk about it, to go into silence, and this can prolong grief.

Even though the article is in context to working in the area of loss and grief, there are parallels in working in sexual assault. Many people I have consulted with had been silenced for a number of years in fear of uncovering painful experiences, which arguably contributed to further silencing of the person from speaking the truth of their experiences of sexual violence, enabling shame to have the last say on matters about their identity. Within narrative practice, while we always wish to provide a place to speak of the negative effects of the clients' experiences of sexual violence, like shame, we are also interested in hearing about how people have stayed connected to more preferred ways of acting/being. This is about making it possible to talk about the effects of the experiences of sexual violence in honouring ways (Wingard 2011).

A common thread to the stories I have witnessed, whether that be a survivor of sexual violence or a parent/carer of a child who has survived sexual violence, is guilt and/or shame – for example, *'what they had done'* regarding an adult survivor referencing the sexual violence they had experienced as a child; and '*I should have known*' in reference to a parent whose child had experienced sexual violence. To develop an understanding of Dale's shame, it was important to invite Dale to consider how shame had silenced his values and beliefs. Hearing what people give value to creates a foundation for collaboration. Through this mode of enquiry, additional externalising conversations made it possible for Dale to gain further distance from taking on shame as part of his identity conclusion. The model Alan Jenkins presented in his book *Invitations to responsibility* was then adapted into our work together (1990). Instead of looking at the situation from the perspective of the person who carried out the sexual violence as Alan Jenkins did, I examined the experience of shame from the perspective of the person experiencing the sexual violence. This way of positioning myself brought with it an assumption that to tell a story is, inescapably, to take a moral stance. The way we narrate our lives shapes what they become. That's their power and what it means is, if we can change our stories, then we can change our lives. I was hoping to make visible to Dale that his experience of shame wasn't a pervasive judgement of himself and what he had done; alternatively, his shame could be associated with the realisation that it was the person who carried out the sexual violence who had acted in a dishonourable way – hence, promoting a realisation that Dale's personal integrity was being challenged through these dishonourable acts (Jenkins 2007, 419). These conversations contested Dale's ideas around his personal shame. Finding a safe passage that enables pathways into the person's journey towards allowing for shame to be understood and addressed in ways that promote personal agency can be extremely difficult, because of shame's influence and silencing effects (Jenkins 2007).

Exploring Dale's values and beliefs and how he defined them, for himself, allowed me to identify what was important to Dale, enabling further externalising conversations to occur. When shame was broken and understood as a recognition of value awareness, it allowed for the sexual violence to be talked about, thus creating an environment for Dale where he was no longer silenced. During our walk together, Dale and I were able to come to an understanding that, without the shame, there is a realisation that it is better to talk about the sexual violence, as the stories of abuse need to be shared and released from the person. These conversations can then be spoken about out loud and shared for public view. This doesn't take away from the fact that the sexual violence has played a major part in shaping how the person sees themselves. It enables further breaking of shame and for the person to put the sexual violence into perspective – for example, it is not their fault. Before Dale and I were able to talk about shame in this way, it was crucial in our therapeutic journey to explore his ideas of self that were informed by the negative effects he had experienced from the abuse. Early on, many of our conversations focused on trying to make meaning of Dale's experiences. I have included part of a transcript from our first session, highlighting some of these negative effects and introducing ideas around externalising conversation.

TIM: *So tell me more about what brings you here.* (After Dale shared about the effect of writing his victim impact statement.)

DALE: ... *the mixed emotions since receiving the phone call wanting me to write a victim impact statement.*

TIM: *Tell me more?*

DALE: *Life changed from that point on, after the incident in front of the boys at school ... it's not who I am, how people think I am, like being called Ridsdale's bum-boy. After the incident not knowing what it was, to be me.*

TIM: *How has this affected you if you could name it ... umm... could you name the effects this incident has had on you?*

DALE: *These feelings have been resurfaced – like the feelings of not coping and from that, crying a lot of the time.*

TIM: *Are you okay if we unpack this idea of 'crying a lot' that informs your ideas that you are not coping. What I am trying to say is that society often dictates how we perceive this idea of crying. Generally, it is seen as a negative emotion, a weakness by society, to see a man crying. Yet, what is it like to see your acts of crying as an indication of hurt, and the tears experienced being a protest against something important to you that has been taken away?*

Externalising conversations involve deconstructing people's ideas of the problem and how they are informed. The way in which we use language determines our relationship with problems. This, in turn, establishes the courses of action available to us in attempting to lessen the effects of the problem on our lives. One idea Dale and I explored was placing 'the' in front of the problem as a way to externalise, in the context that 'the problem is the problem, the person isn't the problem.' (White 2007). This enabled Dale and I to look at the problem objectively. Dale was able to think about the problem stories in his life with clarity and conviction, enabling a further breaking away from being silenced. Further to this, Dale was given a reflective space to be able to gain a unique understanding of 'the crying' where it was not purely viewed as a problem but an indication of what was important to him

16 *Revealing and grasping the coat*

being compromised. Dale and I were able to move the conversation in a direction that explored his understanding of the way he lives, based on his past history of experiences, which identified his beliefs of the world he continued to hold onto.

DALE: *It's okay ... there are feelings of conflict with what I grew up to believe ... feelings of being compassionate and supportive, which goes against my feelings that I now have of shame, fear, embarrassment, hate for what he did. The hate – it is always bubbling away, and the confusion around this because I don't like hatred, but I'm also having those feelings regarding the boys for their bullying of me after the incident.*

TIM: *So there are times that you did know who you were?*

DALE: *I guess ... he had no right to do that* [referring to the person that carried out the sexual violence].

TIM: *So, what ... who do you value in your life?*

DALE: *My family ... it is nice to have their support and this allows me to go on ... it gives me strength and that is a good feeling – feeling refreshed, unburdened. They know me.*

TIM: *So, when was the last time someone in your family showed you that they knew who you really were?*

DALE: *My daughter ... she wrote a letter to me.*

TIM: *Was the letter typed ... handwritten or ... ?*

DALE: *Handwritten.*

TIM: *Wow ... what did this mean to you?*

DALE: *It meant a lot.*

TIM: *Was there anything in the letter that stood out for you?*

DALE: *There was ... in the letter she mentioned what a strong person I am and she thanked me for loving them and being caring.*

TIM: *Was there anything else that reflected who you are as a person?*

DALE: *She also wrote that I brought her up with good values, values of strength, openness and talking things through.*

Dale was now able to challenge these long-held negative ideas of how he saw himself and experience another layer to his identity that wasn't only defined by his experiences of sexual violence. Dale and I were able to look at alternate storylines, honouring him above his experiences of sexual violence.

During our conversations, it was particularly important to create an environment that promoted the capacity for Dale to identify the power relations behind the dishonourable acts that had determined him, influencing the effects of shame in his life (Jenkins 2007). An inquiry into someone's experiences of sexual violence that solely focuses on the chemical responses in their brain, or the judgement turned against the 'self', or cognitive distortions of thinking – and leaves out conversations about a client's values and beliefs around the effects of power relations on the basis of gender, race or sexuality – can be accused of failing to understand the construction of the psychological problems in social contexts. Michel Foucault considers the ways in which people are active in 'crafting' or negotiating their identity (Danaher and Webb 2000, pp. 116–118):

> People are not free agents who make their own meanings and their thoughts are scripted by social forces and institutions and relations of power.... Where, rather than being the free and active organisers of society, we are products of discourses and power relations and take on different characteristics according to the range of subject positions that are possible in our socio-historical context.

4 The politics of men's pain

Informing our 'walking alongside' each other

Key points to consider

- <u>Men's ways of being</u>: *Challenging dominant images of masculinity.*

Early on in my work with Dale, I was curious in exploring dominant discourses influencing 'what it is to be male' and what ideas around men's ways of being are for the adult men who have experienced sexual violence. These ponderings were in relation to wanting to understand shame and how dominant masculinities played into the silencing of Dale's experiences. At the time, I was asked the question: 'Are we talking about what it means to be male or are we talking about hegemonic masculinity?' (Denborough, personal communication 2016).

Hegemonic masculinity could be described as the maintaining of the dominance of societal roles over women and other gender identities. These representations promote stereotypes that support masculine heterosexual values.

The stories men tell themselves about their pain will largely determine the action they take in an attempt to improve their lives. As McLean et al. explore in *Men's ways of being* (1996), the 'claim that men are oppressed too' places men and women on an equal footing and removes the need to face up to fundamental power differences structured along gender lines. A denial of male pain, on the other hand, conflicts with men's actual experience of themselves. Throughout Western history, there have been a number of dichotomies which have been very powerful in shaping images of masculinity. They operate as restraints against changes men might make. These splits in shaping men's view of themselves can be seen to inform many of the injustices that have occurred throughout the centuries. Arguably this informs much of the sense of alienation and confusion many men experience today.

During my 'walking alongside' Dale, we were able to deconstruct many of the negative effects that were influencing him, from being silenced for forty-two years. As Dale began to reclaim what was already his and develop a deeper understanding of shame, he was able to resist these negative effects of hegemonic masculinity and speak the truth about his experiences of sexual violence. During this process it was important to acknowledge that Dale's subjective experience of personal suffering was real and he was not alone; many other men have experienced the pain of oppressive acts against them and been silenced due to dominant discourses

DOI: 10.4324/9781003256816-5

surrounding masculinity. Growing up in a world that entertained and implicitly encouraged a certain way of operating always felt 'unnatural' to me. For instance, if your rational thoughts were not given precedence over your emotions, this implied there wasn't any clear reasoning behind your decision making. Therefore, this has the effect of your judgement being questioned by yourself and others, with doubt getting thrown upon your end decision (McLean et al. 1996). What has become apparent is that what I am working towards, and at times feel as though I am working against, is understanding those dominant discourses around what masculinity actually means. Working in collaboration with Dale has made this book, *Reclaiming lives from sexual violence,* possible. During our time together, we have been able to challenge the dichotomies surrounding men's ways of being, which has allowed for Dale's direct experiences of sexual violence to be shared and spoken about.

5 Deconstructing negative identity conclusions

Key points to consider

- <u>Further detailed externalising conversations</u>: *Generating space where positive identity conclusions can be talked about.*
- *Richly describing the client's life that isn't defined by the silencing effects of the problem.*
- *Enabling deconstruction of the power practices of the perpetrator.*

Externalising represents just one possibility of many in a range of practices informed by narrative therapy. Externalising isn't a requirement of narrative therapy, and in fact, externalising conversations are not always present in the conversations I have with people who consult me. Yet they can be useful in unpacking some of the negative identity conclusions people bring with them into therapy (White 2001). A more detailed explanation of externalising conversations is referred to in Appendix B.

At the outset of my journey with Dale, he shared with me some of the negative identity conclusions he held about himself – about who he was and what his life was about – and that he was secretly in agreement with. He believed that these conclusions spoke the truth about his identity. When we were three to four sessions into 'walking alongside' each other, we experienced some shared sense developing – that these conclusions didn't speak to the totality of who Dale was. He also had an identity that was somehow separate from, and that even contradicted, these negative conclusions. These negative conclusions no longer represented the total truth of who he was (White 2001).

Over a period of three sessions in 2015, when Dale and I initially started consulting with each other, Dale came to the conclusion 'that I am a person with integrity. I've been closed for a long time, and I'm now allowing myself to be honest … I will keep sharing … previously I couldn't go there as a protection and to be able to function'. Dale was able to talk about the beliefs he had about himself that didn't reflect these new ideas of self. While Dale reflected on his hard-won living skills, he was able to share that previously during the abuse, 'not being how others have seen me' for instance, 'the name-calling and bullying during the time of violent childhood sexual abuse, put me in a place of uncertainty and confusion about who I am. Now I am more informed, I know the truth, so I can be honest

DOI: 10.4324/9781003256816-6

Deconstructing negative identity 21

underneath all that shame and fear, realising that who I was will always be part of who I am now, that that part of me didn't die, and that's a good thing'.

With my assistance Dale was supported to break from long-held negative identity conclusions, which paved the way for the introduction of other conversations that contributed to the exploration of, and generation of, more positive identity conclusions. These positive identity conclusions were not stand-alone for Dale – they were associated with his specific knowledge of life and practices of living (White 2001).

TIM: *What part of you died that day?* (referring to the sexual violence)

DALE: *I felt my innocence had been taken away, it died ... the effects of that are guilt. I hadn't lost that innocence beforehand.*

TIM: *Why's that important to you?*

DALE: *Because there's a lot of me in that ... that innocence ... and there still is.*

TIM: *What's the innocence about?*

DALE: *The young boy, who hadn't experienced anything like that before ... I felt older, always felt older since then ... I had a taste of feeling young, I wasn't young for long enough.*

TIM: *How does this affect you now?*

DALE: *It's devastating, scary ... I know as an adult now, I was innocent in all that and everyone else made me guilty, when referring to the bullying and the feelings of judgement.*

TIM: *What are some of the effects of telling someone for the first time?*

DALE: *Good to tell someone. Someone else knows.*

TIM: *Do you hold onto that innocence now and what does this say about what you value as a person?*

DALE: *Yes, I have to ... that's the bit that was dead, hanging onto it makes me realise I'm still here. Now I know I was innocent; the innocence is being resurrected and now the openness of being able to share, the release, and the honesty in me is coming out.*

TIM: *Are there any other ways that you could name 'the innocence is being resurrected'?*

DALE: *'The protest' is getting stronger ... the brokenness is okay – got to go through it.*

Dale was then invited to deconstruct these negative ideas about how he viewed himself in conversation, which was when the process of externalising conversations began. The Statement of Position maps have supported my practice through a subtle weaving of questions of curiosity (White 2007). Statement of Position maps externalise the problem, enabling the conversation to acknowledge the full effects of the problem on a person's life, whether positive, negative or in between. The person can then distance themselves from the immediacy of the problem, thus identifying a non-problem place for them to stand in (refer to Appendix B for more on Statement of Position maps). The weaving of effects and evaluation questions that rely on the expert knowledge of the person moves the problem out of the realm of expert professional knowledge and back into a realm within which the person's own solutions can be utilised (Mann and Russell 2002, p. 5). Dale and I focused on his honesty and how sharing his truths from what he experienced was contradicting the previously held belief that the sexual violence was his fault.

22 *Deconstructing negative identity*

TIM: *As you have made mention previously, if we are able to name the honesty, as a protest against the dishonesty* [of the institution and their lack of compassion], *if that's okay with you. When has the honesty made a stand for Dale? Does this make sense?*

DALE: *Well … recently when talking to my school friend Robert over the phone.* [Robert had also experienced sexual violence.]

TIM: *What does this say about who you are … your identity … from this action you took* [the honesty] *with the protest against the dishonesty?*

DALE: *I guess … that I am open, can let people in; let them know where I am coming from.*

TIM: *How does this affect you, knowing what you know about 'the honesty' that is in your life?*

DALE: *I guess that is who I am, part of who I am … 'the honesty'.*

TIM: *You have talked about the shame from what you have experienced. How does this play into 'the honesty' that we have been chatting about?*

DALE: *What people think I am … trying not to worry about it, too much!*

TIM: *How has this 'trying not to worry about it too much' affected you?*

DALE: *Realising that I am sharing these things, being more open. I don't really mind anymore, feeling vulnerable … I know what being accepted means.*

TIM: *So, what does this mean … this 'being accepted'?*

DALE: *I am accepted by some family members, close friends who I have shared my story with, and they have also shared their history of abuse with me … allowing myself to be vulnerable has allowed them to be vulnerable … which has affirmed that the trust, the acceptance is there.*

TIM: *How is this affecting you now? I mean … sharing this with me for the first time?*

DALE: *… that I am a person with integrity. I've been closed for a long time, I'm now allowing myself to be honest. I will keep sharing … I hope my story can help someone else in the future.*

TIM: *What name would you put to the 'keep sharing'?*

DALE: *Making a stand … yeah, that's what I would name it … the 'keep sharing'.*

Significantly, our work was evolving into a more collaborative effort. Through externalising practices that enabled an objectifying view of the problem story Dale presented with, there was an opening up of our conversations, which gave opportunity to be further understood, and talked about with greater meaning (White 2007). It was then possible to associate the problem story with the acts of sexual violence, which resonated with Dale's experiences and not my expert analysis of the problems in Dale's life. We were then able to talk about the effects of the abuse and introduce the politics of power in the acts, rather than the perceived reality about Dale's own identity (Mann and Russell 2002).

TIM: *So … last session we chatted about the 'keep sharing' and 'making a stand'.*

DALE: [holding a typed letter] *I have written the letter for the lawyer … I've been really emotional at the moment … I am 'facing it head on' and it's not really easy.*

TIM: *Who is the letter for?*

DALE: *I wrote it for myself. I need to share … tell those things?*

TIM: *What does this letter represent for you … ummm … who you are?*

DALE: *Strangely, I felt like it was a lie … I haven't taken the time to write the stuff down before … how it felt.*

Deconstructing negative identity 23

TIM: *How has writing this letter now affected you in making a stand for 'the honesty' and the 'keep sharing'?*

Conversation then centred on how Dale hadn't told his wife the full story of his experiences of sexual violence until that point.

DALE: *For a long time now, I have felt like I have been pretending; it's someone else and this stopped me from dwelling on it ... allowed me to get up every day.*
TIM: *Is this a good thing ... bad thing or both? What do you think?*
DALE: *Well ... it's a good thing.*

Significantly, the power practices of the person who carried out the sexual violence were then briefly discussed in the context of how they had influenced Dale from not sharing the truth with his wife – for instance, Dale's fear of not being believed. It wasn't until later on in our walk that Dale and I were able to further deconstruct these power practices. These conversations are explained in more detail in Chapter 6. Placing Dale's knowledge and experiences at the centre of our conversations was particularly important, as the operations of power had been an influence in silencing him from trusting his own knowledge and judgement – for instance, the feelings of shame and blame that disrupted his life.

TIM: *So ... when we go back to your words, in 'making a stand' and us chatting about the effects on your integrity, including honesty, with the silencing practices of the experiences of the sexual violence. Are we able to talk about your responses to what happened ... implying that you know what it is to not be silenced? For instance, what did you do, in your words to 'make a stand' against what happened?*
DALE: *I put up a fight ... wriggled till I got away. I was fighting for my life.*
TIM: *Are you okay if we now explore other times that you employed 'making a stand' – or can we call it 'putting up a fight'?*

Building upon previous conversations, Dale and I were now centred on thickening up these alternative accounts of him taking action when the experiences of sexual violence occurred, rather than talking about the impacts which could be disabling and potentially further silencing. It was then that three more actions of Dale's were named, identifying where he had 'made a stand' and 'put up a fight' for himself and other family members prior to, during, and after the sexual abuse. Thus, this process of externalising conversations played a significant role in opening up space for further conversations with Dale that contributed to the generation of more positive identity conclusions. Furthermore, these conversations that Michael White refers to as 're-authoring conversations' contributed to the rich description of Dale's life that wasn't defined by the silencing effects of shame (White 1995). This rich description of Dale's life and relationships generated possibilities for action in the world that were not previously visible. It is in these 're-authoring conversations' that people step into other experiences of their identity (White 2007). These claims contradicted those associated with the problem-saturated story of his life. Dale had the opportunity to speak of the connection between sharing

24 *Deconstructing negative identity*

his story with his friend Robert and some of the significant purposes and values of his life, and to identify those figures of his history that he was linked to in these. As our conversations continued, the knowledges of life and practices of living associated with these pledges, purposes, values and longings of Dale's become more richly described (White 2005).

Before inviting a client into reclaiming what was already theirs, looking into how they responded to the sexual violence adds to them having the last say on matters about their identity. This is done in a way that allows the person to identify skills and abilities in their responses to the abuse rather than looking solely at the impacts the abuse had on them. Being aware of and attentive to the pain the person has experienced with the sexual violence during these conversations creates safety and a recognition that the pain is always there and cannot be forgotten. This involves checking in with the person on many occasions to see whether they are sitting okay with the, at times, difficult questions of curiosity being asked (Yuen 2007). When a client's positive identity conclusions about themselves is built upon, it is then that detailed conversations regarding the abuse are able to occur, when the timing is right for the person. Furthermore, many years after my therapeutic journey with Dale he was able to share the following:

> Ensuring that the client is not vulnerable to re-traumatisation when talking about what they had experienced is not possible. There should not be such concern for the practitioner of re-traumatising the client. An important part of the therapeutic process is to be able to sit with the person's experiences of trauma which is garrisoned by shame. If the trauma is not experienced again and observed, it cannot be put into perspective, and shame will control the trauma. Shame then continues to have control over the client, keeping them silent.

Dale then went further and shared this insight with me:

> Now we [Tim and I] have a deeper understanding of the way shame works, I want to face each trauma head on – shame is a barrier I can now fight through. My hope is that all practitioners would have a deep understanding of the way shame works and would be great advocates of pursuing clients to push through the shame barrier and face the truth. This does not bring healing, but freedom is gained for the client, through understanding shame, breaking the silence, and speaking the truth out loud, and openly, for others to hear, observe and understand.

The recounting of a client's experiences of abuse is challenging and painful. Acknowledging the person's values and beliefs when having these conversations is crucial to separating the abuse from the person's (secretly) long-held beliefs about themselves that have in many instances informed the shame. When 'walking alongside' Dale he was able to articulate the following:

> I don't think you can separate the abuse from the person. You can, however, pull it out of the memory bank, walk and talk through it, but it is not separated;

Deconstructing negative identity 25

and the long-held beliefs that inform the shame after talking about and walking through the painful memory can take years to come to terms with.

At this point, my role was to draw out these painful memories through our conversation, in a way that relied on Dale's Christian values around standing up for what's right, thus allowing him to shift the belief that the abuse was his fault. Dale was then able to push through the shame, saying:

To break the silence, there's amazing freedom being able to talk about it.

Furthermore, he went on to say:

We are who we are because of all those experiences, and sometimes the only way to protect yourself is to not fight against the perpetrator's evil acts. I found if you fight you get more physically hurt, and you realise how deep the hurt is.

Therefore actions that are linked to what the person is committed to, for instance, protection of self, which hasn't been silenced during the abuse, offers another possibility in their meaning making. These new stories provide understanding of what is important to the person and how they protected themselves from further harm during the abuse, which may not have been talked about before. This guides the questions – so the client can speak about and re-evaluate what they went through, thus allowing them to look at their experiences differently. Additionally, the thinking around 'acts of resistance' empowered Dale to recognise how he had used his skills and abilities to take control over the acts of sexual violence – for instance, his ability to keep himself safe from further harm by not fighting back – thus presenting the idea that Dale *did* have some power over the circumstances, even though he may initially have seen it as letting the abuse happen.

I learnt the hard way when trying to resist Ridsdale, resisting him made him angry, which was so much more frightening because he became violent in his actions of abuse; he was so scary, if I tried to resist him, he hurt me more; if I didn't resist him, even although I hated his every action, he was more caring. It's all really sick, isn't it? And I learnt very quickly that it was better for me not to resist him at all. But no matter what he did, it was painful in many ways, but I was a kid, and I guess I used my integrity, values and my childish knowledge, to understand, if I didn't resist, it would be better for me.

Thus, when we are able to get to a point in conversation where the person is taking action and responsibility for their values and beliefs, it is then that amazing stories of resistance begin to emerge, where 'rich story development' now becomes possible (Yuen 2007). It is in the practice of rich story development that the people we walk alongside come to new and preferred ways of experiencing their lives. It is this preferred storyline that provides the person's own answers and solutions to what is problematic. Furthermore, connection-making questions and conversations put Dale more in touch with his own skills and knowledges (Yuen 2007). Dale was

26 Deconstructing negative identity

able to richly describe his own responses to the abuse, and what these responses, skills, and knowledges may reflect. These conversations did not happen by chance and relied upon a conversational partnership of trust and openness. In the following conversation, Dale and I were able to richly describe the importance he was able to place on being aware of people who are hurting, highlighting actions he took in response to the abuse.

TIM: *When we chat about your responses to the experiences of sexual violence and its effects, how has this effected your 'making a stand' … and 'putting up a fight' in a positive way?*

DALE: *Compassion for people … after going through what I went through … allowed this … hated losing my childhood, in my mind … become a person who looked deeper at people … more aware of people that are hurting.*

TIM *When was the first time you recognised this 'compassion for people'?*

DALE: *The first time I recognised this was at school … there were a few kids not liked at school … there was more to them than that … I looked deeper … past the tears, skin … deep stuff.*

TIM: *How does this affect you … reflecting on your experiences at school and recognising 'the compassion for people' back then?*

DALE: *They* [the kids] *some of them got to know me as well … which made it very special …*

TIM: *What did you learn about who you are from those experiences?*

DALE: *I learnt that we had let each other in.*

When describing and demonstrating the usefulness of externalising conversations, I have shown the extent to which these conversations can contribute to the unpacking of people's negative identity conclusions. These thin conclusions are then deprived of the truth status that has been assigned to them, and they cease to carry the authority they once had. This outcome was readily apparent in the externalising conversations I had with Dale (White 2005).

As White suggested (2005, 2007), re-membering conversations can be used to enrich a person's history. As the following conversation between Dale and myself shows, focusing on how he showed compassion for people and was an honest person enriched his history, allowing him to counter long-held truths around dishonesty and pretending with his wife, by not sharing the full story of his abuse until now. Re-membering conversations enable purposeful engagement with a significant figure in a person's history, allowing a person to challenge the thin conclusions they may have held onto.

TIM: *Who wouldn't be surprised to hear you talk about 'compassion for people' in your life in this way?*

DALE: *It was a friend of mine in early high school.*

TIM: *Did you share particular activities or ideas?*

DALE: *We shared experiences of hurt.*

TIM: *Would you say that they contributed something to your life?*

DALE: *I felt accepted and they were interested in me.*

Deconstructing negative identity   27

TIM: *What did they know about you?*

DALE: *They knew that I cared.*

TIM: *What do you think it meant to them with you being in their life?*

DALE: *They could be themselves.*

TIM: *What did you bring to their life?*

DALE: *I gave them quality time. I brought them some joy; there were a lot of fun times.*

TIM: *If they were in the room, what would they be doing … is there anything they'd like to say about Dale?*

DALE: *She would be sharing also, about our experiences. She would also be smiling.*

TIM: *What would you say to her, now, if they were in the room?*

DALE: *I would thank Rosemary for her acceptance, allowing me to be me; Rosemary could be who she was too.*

TIM: *Is there anything else?*

DALE: *It shows there was some good stuff, growing up.*

TIM: *Tell me more about the good stuff?*

DALE: *The experience of 'the freedom', which was incredible, I wasn't judged.*

TIM: *Are you able to think about these responses and how they were related, if at all to the sexual violence? Please let me know if this is too difficult.*

DALE: *The skills of non-judging others, I was a deeper thinker after the abuse … a good thing that came out of it … a survival thing. During the time* [when at school], *I had to challenge myself in getting up in the morning to go to school … learning new skills to enable me to survive, i.e. being observant, locking it away. It's not easy to try and re-invent yourself … not trying to be someone else. I want people to be able to unlock who they are.*

TIM: *Are these gifts that you now have … the qualities of compassion for people, your strong faith, looking after the well-being of others? These are my words.*

DALE: *I would agree.*

TIM: *Was today's session useful?*

DALE: *It's painful to think about what happened, but it's nice to realise there were some positive times during that time* [of the abuse and ridicule from the students at school].

TIM: *What does this say about who you are … what I mean is, what you value and what your beliefs are?*

DALE: *That I am an honest person … not telling my wife the full story … about the dreams regarding my abuse mucked with the honesty.* [In reference to sharing the letter to his lawyer with his wife.]

Next in our ongoing conversation, it was crucial to acknowledge the actions Dale was taking in sharing with me and the vulnerability it took for him to open up in our conversations. The metaphor of diving into a swimming pool for the first time was used, and furthermore, sitting on the edge of the pool waiting to dive in, not knowing what might lie beneath the surface of the water. By using these images, I hoped to make visible to Dale the trust involved in these actions, where the fear attached could be more richly described and understood. Metaphors are often used in narrative practice, and I was hoping to shift the paradigm from the structuralist idea of implying that something was 'needing fixing' with Dale. For this reason, the

28 *Deconstructing negative identity*

metaphor of diving into a swimming pool was used to socially construct a storyline that Dale could run with, relating this idea to his own lived experiences.

TIM: *When we talk about the diving into unknown waters for the first time, and reference this back to the 'not sharing' your dreams, your story with your wife. What does this tell us about what you was happening for you?*

DALE: *I guess ... what I was doing was protecting myself, until I was ready to dive in and share my story.*

TIM: *Is there anything that you will take away from today ... what I mean is, something that you haven't thought about before today.*

DALE: *I will look at it differently* [regarding the not sharing of his story and it being a protective measure] *... I've been emotionally swaying, being vulnerable, thinking it's crazy putting myself through this* [i.e. not sharing my story because of not wanting to feel vulnerable] *... I think I've done the right thing ... at least telling my wife ... [my] gut feeling ... [is that I've] done the right thing. I'm now feeling a bit happier about it ...*

TIM: *What will we be seeing from you, looking at it differently and facing it head on, with this newfound knowledge of yourself?*

DALE: *I will go home and clean the house ... it's been a couple of months since I have ...*

TIM: *What will this action of cleaning the house indicate to your wife?*

DALE: *She will see some life in me.*

6 Exposing the coat of shame and fighting to claim what is already yours

Key points to consider

- <u>Seeing the problem as an indication of value awareness</u>: *Gaining a deeper understanding of the problem and weakening its control.*
- <u>Enabling reinterpretation of the client's experiences</u>: *Separating the perpetrator's actions from the client's ideas of self through the questions asked.*

As a result of the previous conversations Dale and I shared, his compassion for people was becoming more visible. Significantly, steps Dale had taken in being honest and protecting himself from further harm were founded on his past and present actions, and not my expert analysis. The hard-won knowledges gained through these actions highlighted Dale's commitment to these reclaimed ideas of self, which made it possible for him to share his truths about the sexual violence. Dale's positive identity conclusions were thickened and built upon by him being able to recount actions that he had taken and how he had positively responded to the abuse. What was now made possible was that the abuse did not have the power that it once had. Even though the abuse changed Dale, the shame experienced from the actions of the perpetrator no longer defined how he viewed himself. Distance was gained from views of himself that were totalising and controlling. Dale gained agency to speak about the abuse and its effects. He was now reclaiming his values and beliefs and how the acts of the person who carried out the sexual violence had compromised what he stood for. Dale was beginning to gain a deeper understanding of shame and was able to attempt separating himself from the acts perpetrated against him.

Significantly, Dale was able to see the shame within its social context and not as an internalised view of self, so it was possible to then explore what Dale wanted to make of his life. Finding a safe passage that established an enabling context, which allowed for shame to be understood and addressed in ways that promoted a sense of agency, was carefully navigated (Jenkins 2007). Therefore a safe environment was required, so that shame could be repositioned from a restraining experience to an enabling experience. Recognising that shame was an indication of Dale's value awareness and his knowledge of right and wrong. In addition, when assisting Dale to be in a position of being able to engage in such conversations, I adapted

DOI: 10.4324/9781003256816-7

30 *Exposing the coat of shame and fighting*

questions that Alan Jenkins used when working with men who had been sexual abusers. These questions had an intention of separating the shame from Dale's long-held ideas about himself, which promoted he was in some way to blame for what happened (Jenkins 1993). I was also committed to separating the person who carried out the actions of sexual violence from Dale's ideas of self, by making visible Dale's past actions that aligned with his ethics of care. Until this point I had been 'walking alongside' Dale for thirteen sessions.

TIM: *How are you different from the person who carried out the sexual violence?*

DALE: *This question has brought back some of the memories of the child sexual violence and allowed me to start thinking how different I am to the Catholic priest who carried out the sexual violence. I was brought up to respect others, like my dad, who was an amazing human being.*

TIM: *Did the person who carried out the sexual violence think more about himself or others?*

DALE: *He was the one pushing all this 'his desires', he was the one ... he was the one that made all the moves.*

TIM: *Is the person who carried out the sexual violence a person who could face up to his own problems, or did he just blame others?*

DALE: *The things he said to me as a child made me feel differently – like it was my fault.*

TIM: *In what ways are you different to the person who carried out the sexual violence?*

DALE: *I was a child ... he was an adult and he knew better. He was in a position of trust and authority, and he took advantage of the situation with me. When I was his age, I was working and had a family with young children.*

TIM: *How are your ways of doing things different from his ways?*

DALE: *There was falseness about him, a betrayal of trust ...*

Dale then revealed that this was the first time he had reflected about what happened in this way.

DALE: *I thought he was someone that cared ... it makes me be honest about how he was ... hate for him now. I was brought up to respect people.*

TIM: *Was today's conversation useful?*

DALE: *It unleashes it ... somehow it seems to help with the heaviness, the shame ... lightens it, which is a good thing.*

Furthermore, Dale was invited to take responsibility for his values and beliefs, which had been silenced through his experiences of sexual abuse. On a continuum, we storied the effects of the sexual violence, which were mapped commencing with 'denial' moving through to 'blame', 'guilt' and 'shame', and eventually getting to a point in the conversation where Dale was in a position to consider the idea of taking action to reclaim his values and beliefs. At this time, Dale named 'integrity' as a quality he was reclaiming, and he identified that he was now able to stand up for his values and knowing the difference between right and wrong. Dale's integrity was becoming more visible, where it was shame being silenced, not Dale himself any longer. This was enabling him to speak about his experiences of sexual violence with a commitment to sharing the truth.

Exposing the coat of shame and fighting 31

When referring to Dale's values, to quote Michael White (1995, p. 58): 'I was referring to values with a small 'v'... and not those that establish some normalising judgement of the person ... I was referring to an ethical position'. Dale took an ethical position during his childhood experiences and continued to take them moving towards living life in his preferred way. It was now a possibility to move the conversation to where the shame began to separate from how Dale saw himself. Following is an example of the reclaiming integrity framework I used with Dale (Table 6.1).

Differentiating a client's relationship with shame from what they hold value to in life is not always easy. These internalised judgements are very strong and as White says (1995, p. 42–43):

> when we look at the history of the world's cultures, modern internalised discourses have provided for quite a novel way of thinking about and speaking about oneself and others. They have the effect of isolating persons from each other, and the very contexts of their own lives, which erases context that splits the experience from the politics of local relationships

Consequently, Dale was able to gain a deeper understanding of the effects of shame and break through the silence. Because of this, Dale was inviting himself to undertake and invest in a journey towards responsibility and respect of self. Significantly, the practice of engaging with Dale using this model assisted him to find motivation to discover his own preferences and capacities for respectful ways of being and relating to himself. There were now opportunities for the reinterpretation of Dale's experiences of abuse and for deconstructing further his negative stories of identity. Once Dale's own knowledges of his experiences of sexual violence were established in specific detail, this:

- a) made possible the grounding of adequate testimonies, which were experiences near to Dale
- b) supported Dale to develop a level of thinking that made it possible for him to distinguish those actions that are directed towards him that are exploitative, abusive or neglectful in nature from those actions directed towards him that are compassionate, loving, or caring in nature
- c) opened up the possibilities that are before Dale to take action to resist and to confront these knowledges and practices of shame in his day-to-day life.

(White 2005)

It was then possible to explore how Dale's integrity had been affected by his experiences of sexual violence as well as how the power practices of the person who carried out the sexual violence had silenced Dale's integrity.

Thus, when deconstructing the effects of the sexual violence on Dale's integrity, opportunities presented, enabling Dale to move through the guilt and shame to an acceptance of him being honest with strong moral principles. Significantly, Dale was now able to see shame as an indicator of his humanity that could be acknowledged as an indicator of value awareness (Jenkins 2007), for instance:

32   *Exposing the coat of shame and fighting*

Table 6.1 Invitations to integrity continuum using arrow

DENIAL GUILT SHAME TAKING RESPONSBILITY FOR MY VALUES / BELIEFS		GROWTH IN MY VALUES AND BELIEFS
←		→
Misplacing of my own values and beliefs	Transition into acknowledging my own values and beliefs	Honouring of my own values and beliefs
- I don't know who I am - I could have stopped it - Why didn't I tell anyone until now? - Why did I keep going back to them? - I was told that I brought it on myself - I was always seen as different - No one would have believed me - My physical reaction was repulsive TAKING ON THE ACTS OF THE OPPRESSOR AS YOUR OWN	- Recognising responses to the experiences of oppressive acts i.e. 'acts of resistance' - Talking about my values - Standing up for what's right - Being honest - Putting myself first - Trusting others - Recognising that I am a forgiving person - Recognising that I have protected myself and my family - Talking about the power practices of the person who sexually abused me - Interviewing 'Shame': its power practices and the social context to its influence TRANSITIONING TO RECOGNISING MY VALUES AND BELIEFS	- Understanding more deeply the effects that the experience of oppressive acts has had on me i.e. the good, the bad, the in between - Being honest with people without feeling guilty regarding talking about the oppressive acts - Feeling calm about the decisions I make - Thinking about what my values and beliefs are - Gaining strength in making a stand for what I believe in - Being true to myself i.e. respecting what I believe in - Being open to talking about the confusion regarding the physical reactions to the sexual violence - Understanding the effects of hurt from other people's experiences of oppressive acts HAVING THE LAST SAY ON MATTERS ABOUT MY IDENTITY

This version adapted from the work of Alan Jenkins (1993).

TIM: *How would you describe integrity and what it means to you?*

DALE: *Your ability to recognise whether or not you should be ashamed or whether you should feel comfortable in regards to an action or a situation … having your integrity broken through actions, through forces that are uncontrollable/unforeseeable.*

TIM: *What does the word integrity mean for you?*

DALE: *It's to do with the way I was brought up – my strong Christian values and about reflecting on how I want to be treated. Being honest and working on revealing what is wrong first and then what is right.*

TIM: *What does your integrity say about who you are, as a person?*

DALE: *I can now speak up ... I don't have to be ashamed for what Ridsdale [who carried out the sexual violence] did to me ... it's not my fault ... I've done nothing wrong.*

TIM: *When we try to understand what your values are, how would you define them with regards to the decisions you make?*

DALE: *I have the ability to stick up for what's right and wrong.*

It was now possible for Dale to deconstruct the power practices of the person who carried out the sexual violence. Dale was able to name the effects that the person who carried out the sexual violence had over him, which controlled the silencing of his integrity. During this time, Dale renamed the acts perpetrated against him as 'sexual violence' and in his words 'this is what *it* is – *it* being the act of sexual violence', identifying that the person who carried out the sexual violence as being 'dishonourable to his moral judgement' (Jenkins 2007). Furthermore, Dale shared that naming it as 'acts of sexual violence' was useful when breaking through shame to place these experiences into perspective, which was liberating. Dale shared that prior to being able to externalise 'the sexual violence', he took it on as part of his identity, therefore taking the blame for what happened.

With these newly held beliefs regarding his integrity and the separation of the sexual violence from how Dale saw himself, and with careful consideration and sensitivity, we wrote down on the whiteboard, 'How could the integrity let the sexual violence happen?' My intention was to draw out the power practices of the person who carried out the sexual violence. What was revealed on the whiteboard was the control the person who carried out the sexual violence had in silencing Dale's integrity through their abuses of power. Dale was able to name how he differed from the person, what he stood for and the facts of the circumstances that controlled him during the abuse. Significantly Dale was able to acknowledge that, during the experiences of sexual violence, he was put into a position of powerlessness, physically and emotionally. Following on from this, at the bottom of the whiteboard, Dale clearly articulated how he was gaining some agency in voicing how he no longer believed that the sexual violence was his fault, giving him strength to speak the truth. For Dale to now be able to talk about his experiences in this way enabled future conversations where he was also able to develop a deeper understanding of the control that the person carrying out the sexual violence had. Dale was beginning to have the last say on matters about his identity, not the shame. It must be noted that at this point with Dale, we had been 'walking alongside' each other for fourteen sessions (Figure 6.1).

Allowing Dale to put his own name to the abuse and its effects, rather than talking about our global understanding of the effects of sexual abuse, allowed for greater detail to be included in the conversations where the experiences were personal to Dale, rather than talking in general about sexual abuse. This established Dale's capacity to discern, in his own life, actions that are of a loving nature from

34 *Exposing the coat of shame and fighting*

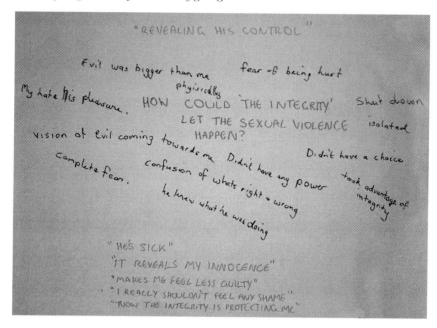

Figure 6.1 Whiteboard notes describing Dale revealing the control of the perpetrator.

actions that are abusive or exploitative (White 2005). Once a client's own experiences of sexual violence are understood and can be talked about freely, as well as the techniques of abuse used by the person that carried out the sexual violence are clearly established, those experiences of the client can be contextualised and linked to the dominant practices of power in our culture – for instance, the history of men's relationship to women, children and to other men in reference to ideas surrounding hegemonic masculinity.

There were now possibilities to explore Dale's relationship between his personal experiences of abuse and how shame has been influenced through society's ideas of what it means to be a man and the stereotypes that come with that. It was now useful for Dale to further deconstruct shame as an externalised emotion, enabling the control of shame to be further weakened and understood.

7 Positioning yourself in ways that acknowledge strength in what you stand for

To know shame, you have to know the Truth.

(Dale Johns 2015)

Key points to consider

- Externalising the problem: *Being aware of the effects of pervasive social discourses and at the same time attending to the particulars of a client's personal experience.*
- Making more visible the client's preferred ways of being: *Beginning to acknowledge a strength in what the client stands for, recognising their ability to push through the problem.*
- Therapeutic letter writing: *Exploring the client's local meanings and ways of understanding life that they bring.*

At this point Dale and I were able to concern ourselves with the need to confront shame, taking into consideration the influences brought about through society's beliefs and assumptions regarding what it means to be male (Winslade 2005). My hope was to bring about social change, yet in my walk with Dale, ethically, it was important to not push my own agenda when carrying the conversations into the political domain without carefully considering Dale's personal experiences. On the other hand, approaches to counselling that do not take notice of the effects of power relations can be accused of failing to understand the production of psychological problems in social contexts, as Winslade suggests. For example, an account of anxiety that solely focuses on chemical changes in the brain can scarcely be considered adequate. Rather than making a pathologising assumption about the origins of the problems, implying a personal deficit in Dale, I sought to locate the problem of shame outside of Dale by entering into the world of discourse and story.

As a consequence, how can counsellors, therapists and practitioners work while being aware of the effects of pervasive social discourses and at the same time attending to the particulars of someone's personal experience? An example of the effectiveness of this consideration can be seen in an interview I had with Dale, where we explored the power practices of shame on his life. The transcript that follows demonstrates a form of externalising conversations. I invited Dale to put himself in the character of being interviewed as 'Shame'. I have found that deconstructing shame in this way can

DOI: 10.4324/9781003256816-8

36   *Positioning yourself in ways*

vary depending on the person I am consulting with. Dale and I had been 'walking alongside' each other for twenty-five sessions at this point. (Refer to Appendix C for the template used during the interview). During this process, care needed to be taken in that I was not imposing my own agenda and the dominant discourses that were talked about belonged to Dale's understandings and not on my own (Winslade 2005).

TIM: *Are you okay if we talk about the shame today?*
DALE: *Okay*
TIM: *What would your definition of shame be… how would you define what shame means for you?*

Dale had commenced the session by referencing the flashbacks, memories and shame he experienced by having woken up having ejaculated.

DALE: *It's an overpowering sense of guilt, which holds hands with shame and takes over. Guilt fights my knowledge of right from wrong, pushing me down the shame pit … covered in the filth of sexual violence, fragile, betrayed, overpowered by the words spoken over me by Ridsdale – my fault, my punishment for the evil things I've done. Shame is broken, but I have a deeper understanding now of the way shame works, shame is powerful and it's a constant fight against my Christian values to keep it at bay. It's been a part of my life… I have tried to deny what happened.*
TIM: *If 'Shame' had a colour what would it be?*
DALE: *Burgundy… it's pretty dark and it's stained with blood.*
TIM: *Are you okay if we now interview Shame. It may feel a little strange and if it gets too difficult just let me know. Are you okay to give it a go and see how it goes, Shame?*
DALE: *Yep… [silent nod].*
TIM: *Tell me about yourself and how you have worked in Dale's life.*
DALE (as SHAME): *I've kept him in a place of guilt and denial…*
TIM: *When did you first come into Dale's life?*
DALE (as SHAME): *I think instantly that first time Dale experienced the sexual violence.*
TIM: *What do you think Dale remembers about his life before you came along?*
DALE: *Shame remembers Dale just being very normal, happy and loved.*
TIM: *What tactics do or did you use to trick Dale?*
DALE (as SHAME): *I lied to Dale. Telling Dale that it was his fault… the sexual violence…*
TIM: *What do you help others to believe about Dale?*
DALE (as SHAME): *They probably know the truth… . It's strange because people seem to see Dale as something he isn't. Shame tells others that Dale is weak, scum, Ridsdale's bum-boy and a poofter.*
TIM: *So, what is the truth that people know about who Dale is? Can you remember what is said to Dale to remind him of that?[1]*
TIM: *How much of Dale's life do you/ or have you taken up?*
DALE (as SHAME): *Most of it…*
TIM: *What is this saying about the times that you haven't taken up Dale's life?[2] Who else stands behind you to help you?*
DALE (as SHAME): *The truth … because of the lies Shame tells Dale. The lies Dale has copped by believing what happened wasn't true. Shame keeps revealing the truth … Shame uses confusion.*

Positioning yourself in ways   37

TIM: *Do you have any allies that you rely on for extra assistance?*

DALE (as SHAME): *Confusion … it all depends what it's about. I guess it's about who Dale is … I tell Dale all the negative things … such as getting the guilt back into Dale's life … the lack of balance between everything. Shame relies upon denial – Dale denying the truth and that it happened. Shame buddies up with the physical reactions, like the ejaculation.*

TIM: *What lies have you been telling – past, present, in the future?*

DALE: *Shame believes that he has kept Dale in a place of never forgetting he is unworthy and scum, and all that filth is there, just sitting there. Shame relies on Dale's Christian values … it's like a game of shame.*

TIM: *How useful are you to Dale?*

DALE (as SHAME): *Not good … because I keep him in a place of confusion … which I like.*

TIM: *What does being in Dale's life say about Shame?*

DALE: *That it only stuffs Dale up… . It keeps Dale in a place of deep sin.*

TIM: *What beliefs do you inspire in Dale?*

DALE (as SHAME): *That it was Dale's fault…*

TIM: *Anything else?*

DALE (as SHAME): *I guess that Shame makes Dale feel like he did something to cause this … Dale must have made himself attractive to it … I remind Dale, it was you that kept on going back.*

TIM: *What plans have you influenced Dale to make?*

DALE (as SHAME): *That Dale controls Shame. That all those decisions to keep going back to Ridsdale's remain, because of Shame – Shame was making Dale go back … Shame thinks that it really took Dale's integrity away and who Dale was. So, I took away what Dale knew of what's right and wrong. I kept Dale there … in a place of unworthiness.*

TIM: *What purpose do you serve in Dale's life?*

DALE (as SHAME): *Destruction of Dale and his integrity and who he is.*

TIM: *Can you remember the time when you left Dale to get on with his life or when you were weaker?*

DALE (as SHAME): *I get weaker when Dale tries to believe that it is not his fault. Also, remembering that the sexual violence is not Dale's fault. When Dale sees the truth … that is knowing that Dale is not to blame … not to blame for the sexual violence.*

TIM: *What will life be like without you, Shame?*

DALE (as SHAME): *I don't know if I know … I can't go back to who I was … Dale hopes it can be better* [for the present and the future] *…it will have to be.*

TIM: *What would Dale like to ask you, if he was in the room?*

DALE (as SHAME): *Nothing. I know Dale very well. Dale would tell me to piss off.*

TIM: *When you think about shame and your influence over Dale, how have other social contexts influenced how you work? Let me see – like the role of Dale's gender, i.e. being male. Does this make sense, Shame?*

DALE (as SHAME): *Yeah … Dale is definitely male … Dale has feared, been bullied by and hasn't been liked by other males much. In Australia, it's pretty much ocker male, which Dale is not – this has influenced me. I tell Dale he isn't an ocker male, so therefore he must be different.*

TIM: *What does Shame say about what it is to be a male in today's world?*

DALE (as SHAME): *Shame doesn't know anymore … part of the confusion I guess. The world's confused … umm … I guess that Dale has experienced the confusion that comes*

38 *Positioning yourself in ways*

> *from Dale not wanting to be like other males from Dale's life experiences and what society says it is to be a man ... most males but not all.*

TIM: *Is Shame aware of any other dominating thoughts that keep them alive in Dale's life?*

DALE (as SHAME): *Definitely, there are many things that keep Shame alive in Dale's life. One of those things is Dale's sexuality; Dale is married but has not been sexually active for over sixteen years. Dale just can't go there, he has no sexual feelings toward anyone. But then the flashbacks and nightmares – Dale can be screaming, sobbing, his body reacts like Dale's just been raped again; the body also reacts with a sexual response. The sexual confusion and the horror of this experience which is totally out of Dale's control, and it's all so amplified because Shame grabs hold of truths like that and has a field day with Dale's emotions. Should Dale feel less male because of this? It makes Dale feel the way society portrays what a male should be ... unachievable for Dale.*

TIM: *Can I now ask Dale, is there anything that you will take away from today's interview with Shame?*

DALE: *I guess it reveals how much Shame has had control ... which is a bad thing. It's all probably stuff that I know, but I will think about in a different way ... just not letting what the world thinks to judge who I am. I need to not let Shame have its way ... I need to stop that ... stop dwelling somewhere I shouldn't be. I have to dismiss it when the first thought of Shame comes my way. Probably change what I am doing at the time ... think about something that is positive. When I have a negative thought, I will try and turn it around instead of wallowing in it. I am going to be very aware of what my mind is doing ... and that's a good thing .... and recognising that it's a rollercoaster ... and that it's okay ... [asking myself] what am I getting so stressed about? It's about my integrity and what society says. Stuff them.*

Interviewing the problem – Shame – in this way aims to help a person free the characteristic attributes of stories that are proving problematic in their life and to reposition themselves in more preferable, alternative ways. A narrative perspective suggests that a person's problems and struggles in life and their resources for dealing with those problems are largely cultural, embedded within the person's moral fibre (Winslade 2005). As practitioners we can work very closely with the person, at times hearing very intimate detail of their life's story. As Winslade wrote (2005, p. 357), we therefore need to 'work with the effects of dominant discourses in their lives and with the discursive qualities that they can gather to re-author preferred stories in their lives, as the basis for going forward'. However, as I have emphasised with my own practice, it is clearly not possible to change a dominant discourse within a single counselling conversation. Foucault refers to a patterned set of meanings and social practices that are established through a multitude of conversations, both written and spoken, across a wide social landscape (Winslade 2005). For these reasons, it is important for the individual to be in charge of their own discourse to have any possibility of shifts in their way of thinking about themselves and how they might live their life. Also, the practice of externalising brings with it a close enquiry of the deeply personal effects of the internalisation of dominant discourse in a person's life. Therefore, by locating the problem outside the person and in the world of intellectual enquiry, any story can bring about conversation that can challenge society, in which injustices and abuses of power occur

Positioning yourself in ways 39

(Winslade 2005). This is not suggesting that the problem is being taken away from the person; it's enabling the conversation to focus on the problem in an objective way, which comes without labels and judgement of who the person is. Through social movement, people develop alternative ways with which to contest the power of dominant discourses. In a person's personal life, they can therefore resist the ways in which they are positioned within these dominant discourses and seek to reposition themselves in a more favourable position, as witnessed at the end of my interview with Dale playing the role of 'Shame' (Winslade 2005).

While developing alternative ways for Dale to contest his experiences of shame and to move in a direction that made more visible his preferred ways of living, Dale was beginning to acknowledge a strength in what he stood for, recognising his ability to push through the shame. Michael White (2002) describes the 'rites of passage' metaphor as offering another frame that can assist the practitioner in meaning making – that is, acknowledging the movement that we experience in the conversations we have with the people who consult us. What White describes as his shared engagement with the person regarding this metaphor contributed to the way I positioned myself in the conversations between Dale and me, allowing for:

a) the presence of mind that was required to give Dale's painful experiences deeper meaning
b) our ability to sit with the uncomfortableness of detail shared during the sessions
c) options for Dale and I to fight back the desire to bring about an early closure of our journey
d) further growth in our ability to respond in ways that fitted with the ethical responsibilities that had been considered in my work with Dale.

Michael White identifies three phases when discerning the 'rites of passage' metaphor that have relevance to my walk with Dale (2002):

- *Separation phase:* When initially consulting with Dale, we started to recognise the effects of shame in his life – for example, the effects of being silenced from sharing his truth for forty-two years.
- *Liminal phase:* Dale then began to recognise the effects from sharing the truth with others, which was foreign and confusing – for example, thoughts such as 'What do people think about me now?' and 'How come I share with some people and not others?'
- *Reincorporation phase:* Dale began recognising that sharing the truth was important to him – and in particular, how this sharing was a fight against the Christian values he had been taught, i.e. to trust the people in positions of power, and how this had kept him silent for all those years. Further, Dale was now able to acknowledge the abuse did happen with clarity and conviction, realising it wasn't his fault.

When considering White's 'rites of passage' metaphor and recognising skills that Dale had learnt along the way that now enabled him to share his truths, we then

40 *Positioning yourself in ways*

interviewed Dale's integrity (refer to Appendix D for another example of this interview). The questions asked made it possible for Dale to experience the sort of compassion for himself that he often experienced for others. The following excerpt leads into Dale being interviewed as his 'Integrity', further highlighting the use of externalising practices.

TIM: *If you were to have some more breathing space from Shame, what kind of person would you be able to be?*

DALE: *I'd be lighter… I think … and happier. I think that's because shame is so heavy … and it changes who you are … who you perceive you are … shame is a liar; I'd be able to live in the truth.*

TIM: *What does this look like?*

DALE: *Somehow the memories of the sexual abuse are ever present, there is so much that can bring it back … and the shame comes back with it. Yet I can fight back now and I am not silent anymore; I can talk about it. That's sort of a freedom from silence.*

TIM: *What have you seen in yourself in moments of freedom from resistance to Shame?*

DALE: *I think it's joy.*

TIM: *Tell me more about that.*

DALE: *It's like getting involved in watching a movie or reading a book that you get right into … you don't think about the shame or the guilt or the heaviness; it's lifted. It has to be a movie you get into … I suppose it's taking you somewhere else out of that place of heaviness.*

TIM: *Was there a moment recently?*

DALE: *Yeah … I watched* Shawshank Redemption. *I felt that freedom for some time. Sometimes the heaviness comes in and out during sad times in a movie or book. Also, planning my daughter's wedding took away that heaviness … escapism.*

TIM: *Is it useful to remember the times of freedom?*

DALE: *Yes it is. The body realises part way through these acts of freedom that this is who I am – that this is who I can be.*

TIM: *What does it say about you that you choose these values over succumbing to Shame?*

DALE: [During these acts of freedom]… *I think I feel like that I can beat it. I can be free from the shame… that's just a mind game, isn't it?*

TIM: *Is it useful to see it in this way?*

DALE: *Yes, it is… it's useful that I should try these acts of freedom more often. What is the game that it is playing … if I let the heaviness go, what does that mean? Deny reality? Or is it … I think hurt comes into it somehow.*

TIM: *Before we interview you, playing the role of Integrity, is it okay to gain an understanding of what integrity means to you?*

DALE: *Yes sure, I've done a little investigation and well, besides Jesus being my saviour and one of the reasons I am still here today, one of the other reasons I am still here fighting on is … because of integrity, and I realise through you counselling me Tim … that in the process we have been through together, you have helped me realise what integrity is… revealing the internal fight that goes on between Shame and Integrity, and just how incredibly hard Integrity has fought to keep me mentally, physically and spiritually afloat, and I realise that Integrity has helped me hold on strongly to my faith in Jesus and my Christian principals. So your question Tim. What does integrity mean to me?*

Positioning yourself in ways 41

> *Integrity has been a major part in my survival of childhood sexual abuse because of the way Integrity fights to make sense of all the struggles I go through on a daily basis, and that Shame and Integrity have very similar power strategies. The difference I believe is … shame is evil and integrity is good and right.*

TIM: *How would you define or explain integrity to me, or to others? I know you have used other words, pictures and images in the past.*

DALE: *Integrity would be a white swan on the water … .it looks like it is gliding over the water, but under the water there's lots going on, its turmoil but the swan just looks like it's floating with ease. Integrity is working hard to get me through the heaviness. I define integrity as the unseen work going on to keep the swan above water.*

TIM: *What is the value of making this meaning?*

DALE: *Because of those feelings of shame and heaviness that I have, Integrity needs to step in and try to overcome those feelings. Hence, the legs and the turmoil underneath the water, this is a representation of how Integrity works.*

TIM: *Which is?*

DALE: *Helps me to see who I can be once the heaviness, turmoil and shame is broken, as Integrity works hard under the water, helping me recognise the way Shame works … understanding shame and how integrity keeps me afloat …*

TIM: *What does this imply?*

DALE: *It gives me hope and a future …*

TIM: *Okay, let's now attempt to interview you as Integrity; let me know if this becomes too confusing or isn't working.*

TIM: *If Integrity had a gender and a colour, what would it be?*

DALE (as INTEGRITY): *I have a gender of my own and I'm just thinking about a colour… the beak of the swan is orange, so I'm saying the colour orange.*

TIM: *Knowing what you now know about yourself, Integrity, is there anything you would like to ask Dale, and how he has affected you, if he were in the room?*

DALE (as INTEGRITY): *I was just thinking … what are you doing Dale? (Tell me more) I would be saying, Dale you give Shame too much power, you are like a yoyo with shame… .stop being like a yoyo… I am here to sort this out, I know the truth about Shame. (The truth, what do you mean?) Shame is always undermining Dale. (Integrity are you stronger or weaker now?) When I can break through Shame's 'power over' Dale I am stronger.*

TIM: *So when we think about the power practices of shame, are you surprised Integrity… about what you've shared?*

DALE (as INTEGRITY): *I am surprised and I'm watching what comes out … it's mind boggling really.*

TIM: *Integrity when looking back at Dale and I walking alongside each other… what does that say about you, and what you stand for? Is your awareness of yourself weaker or stronger now?*

DALE (as INTEGRITY): *Again, I am surprised in a good way… there is a process isn't there. (What does this represent to Dale?) That I am Integrity, I bring strength, honesty and the truth. (What has this taught Dale?) That Dale needs to live with me (Integrity) in his life, and he needs to tell Shame to piss off. (That's an act of resistance isn't it?) Yeah it is.*

TIM: *When Dale first started to come and see me (Tim) for counselling, would you have been surprised to hear Dale talk about himself in this way?*

42   *Positioning yourself in ways*

DALE (as INTEGRITY): *Dale wouldn't have been able to do it, (What do you mean ... about the process?) There's stuff Dale needs to go through... . It gives Dale the ability to have patience sometimes ... there's a lot I have to try and deal with besides shame ... there is fear as well, which is faced in lots of ways, I look at the fear... for example ... the fear of going to sleep... . It shouldn't be a fearful thing, but that puts me into action, I have to start paddling, because going to bed effects Dale in so many ways. Dale fears going to sleep. I know how painful this can be for Dale, there are many things that shouldn't have the power to hurt Dale anymore. But then recently I encouraged Dale to go and sit on the fence at the Inglewood Catholic presbytery, to confront the fear of what happened to him in there, because it can't hurt Dale anymore. (Is this another act of freedom?) Thinking about it ... yes it is. There are all those elements fear, shame and guilt that get in my (Integrity's) way.*

TIM: *What does this say about Dale's value awareness now?*

DALE (as INTEGRITY): *Dale's value awareness improves sometimes, when I (Integrity) win it's much better ... it's in those moments when the heaviness is gone.*

TIM: *What would Dale be doing during these times when heaviness isn't around?*

DALE (as INTEGRITY): *Dale would be enjoying himself, he would be spiritually lighter... he would want to share a coffee and chat with someone, telling a joke, he'd be out of his head space ... he would want to get things done, things he's been neglecting like cooking, cleaning, gardening, and he would be working on writing his book and wanting to get Tim's and his story out to the world. I (Integrity) can stop paddling so fast and be light hearted in those times too. When it's tough and the heaviness is deep, I've got to get those feet moving again; paddling fast for long periods is exhausting ... it can be frustrating for me ... I can be like a stiletto in the back of the head, not letting Dale forget who he is, (with laughter) I try hard ...*

TIM: *When did Dale become aware of what it means to be male in his own life? i.e. Was there anything he was taught as a child ... someone he saw in the school yard, watching on T.V... was there a significant person?*

DALE (as INTEGRITY): *He has always known he is male, but sadly the sexual violence overruled what Dale was taught, and his body's reaction to the nightmares made him ashamed of being male.*

TIM: *What did the sexual violence overrule?*

DALE (as INTEGRITY): *From the sexual violence and the words spoken over him by the perpetrator, the bullying, and the nightmare's overruled and challenged Dale's sexuality, he was confused about what it means to be a male ... but it was more about his sexuality. The sexual violence overruled the things Dale was taught as a male, by his dad, to have strength, but to also show gentleness and love, but Ridsdale's violent sexual acts really shut me (Integrity) down and constantly chipped away at Dale's Christian values challenging his beliefs, all the things his young life was built on. I (integrity) was almost destroyed, I left the room, but what Dale's dad taught him is still there and his Christianity, Dale believes he should be able to live like his dad did, because of his dad's strong example. Dale feels so weak, sinful and filthy most of the time which has a lot to do with me (Integrity) because I push the truth ... so Dale, his Christian values, Shame and I (Integrity) are in a constant struggle, we are like a tumbleweed being tossed and pushed around by Shame, keeping us under his pressure and lies, this puts Dale in the lowest place, then Dale feels and knows just how sinful he is, he doesn't think he can be*

Positioning yourself in ways 43

forgiven, that's a problem for Dale, Dale can't forgive himself, he knows he has been involved in something very sinful. Ridsdale's words over him and the way Dale learnt to protect himself from Ridsdale's violence, makes him believe the sexual violence was his fault. Dale tries hard to fight Shame's power-over that controls him, but when Dale tries to believe his truth and that the sexual violence was not his fault more power is given to me (Integrity).

TIM: *What will it take for Dale to forgive himself or do you, Integrity, need to forgive Dale for what happened?*

DALE (as INTEGRITY): *I don't think Dale knows how to forgive himself, because Shame reminds him all that filth is there, I (Integrity) try and help Dale see the truth, I don't hold anything against Dale, Dale is constantly in turmoil, Dale has his own shame and Ridsdale's shame that's a powerful force fighting against me, I (Integrity) just have to keep pushing the truth. Dale has the courage but he is so mixed up and confused. I'm thanking God Dale met you Tim, I think he is slowly getting to a place where he will see the truth as it really is.*

TIM: *So, when we look at what Dale values in life and what Shame stands in the way of – has this changed throughout the time Dale and I have been walking alongside each other? Does that make sense?*

DALE (as INTEGRITY): *Of course, it has made an enormous difference, it has… there is still some yo-yoing going on between Shame and I (Integrity). I don't think Shame's power will ever stop, but since you Tim … and Dale have been walking alongside each other you have opened Dale's eyes to how Shame works, Dale has a much better understanding of the way Shame works which has now given me (Integrity) a foot in the door to work with you Tim, together we have impacted powerfully on the way Dale sees shame. Dale realises now that Shame stands in the way of everything Dale values in life, thank God for us Tim, we've had to be stubborn and fight to awaken Dale to the truth of his story and how Shame has stubbornly controlled Dale's life. Dale now has the power and ability to fight through Shame's power, with this understanding of shame Dale has the skill to break his silence and talk about his truth.*

TIM: *Thank you Integrity, we will now continue the externalising conversation back now with Dale. Dale are you feeling stronger or weaker now? I mean your sense of who you are – or rather, who you have always been? They are my words.*

DALE: *I am feeling stronger, I have a much better idea about shame and a great understanding of the way shame works, So with Integrity and what I have learnt from you Tim and looking at my father's example, gives me the ability to know that I can do this, I have the support to fight through Shame's power.*

TIM: *Dale, you've mentioned that Integrity has gotten stronger, what's telling you that?*

DALE: *It's having the ability to face my truth, I am so grateful to have your support Tim and it has been paramount to have you walking alongside me … you have also made me understand that Integrity has always been there fighting for me, I have felt lonely and abandoned at times and I think that's because I have had shame and guilt walking alongside me most of my life and not realised Integrity has been the one fighting all along, and I know and understand Integrity's strength now, because I also understand I wouldn't be here today, I wouldn't be alive … if integrity, my faith in Jesus hadn't been so strong.*

TIM: *Dale, who have you recruited along the way regarding your values and beliefs? Who has always been there … that wouldn't be surprised to hear you talk about yourself in this way?*

44   *Positioning yourself in ways*

DALE: *I gained faith/Christian values, strength, stubbornness, integrity and love; together they have played an enormous part in supporting me, which came from thinking about my dad's example by reflecting on how dad lived and survived. I found out just before dad died that dad had been raped by a cousin. Dad was about 16 years old and he and his cousin were rabbiting, dad was at a rabbit borough trying to coax a ferret to come out of the borough, when his cousin pushed dads head down into the entrance of the rabbit borough holding dad there and raping him, after his cousin released dad from his depraved hold over and sexually violent act, he held a gun at dads head for quite some time threatening that if he told anyone ever he would shoot him dead. Dad never knew about what had happened to me, so he will never know what he taught me from looking back at how dad continued to live and be the best example he could be, which would have taken faith, strength, stubbornness/integrity and there has to be God's overruling love and Christian values.*

TIM: *So, what defines you now?*

DALE: *My dad's example is helping me define who I can be, Integrity continues under the water, there's lots going on, lots of recruiting, Integrity has stamina, the water is stirring up a bit, I think it's becoming very clear just how hard Integrity has worked, giving me a way forward.*

TIM: *If you were your own son, what parenting qualities do you think you would be experiencing that would be enriching in your life?*

DALE: *First of all I would be experiencing love, unconditional love …*

TIM: *How does this affect you?*

DALE: *Dad's example gives me the knowledge to know as I picture and look deep into his face and also witnessing how he cared for, nurtured, accepted, and reached out in unconditional love to mum, us children, relatives and many others in the community – that I know I have lived my life with that same attitude and know that if I was my own son I would be loving that child with unconditional love, never judging … . So, it makes me feel safe, nurtured, cared for and understood in and under dad's legacy.*

TIM: *Is there anything that you will take away from this discussion about integrity in our conversation – i.e. words said, a thought, an image?*

DALE: *There is so much I can take away from a conversation like that. I realised when you asked that question (When did Dale become aware of what it means to be male in his own life?) that I have never questioned being male, but understanding I was ashamed of being male, but really it was more about my sexuality because, I am not a sexual person, Ridsdale and his violent sexual acts, took that away from me … which helps me understand myself so much more … and why Integrity felt redundant in that outcome because really Shame won that one. And then the image that came of the swan and how that revealed to me just how hard Integrity has worked to keep me afloat, trying hard to win every outcome.*

TIM: *How does this conversation affect you now?*

DALE: *I think that the interview with Integrity was very eye opening, sessions like that are so important to my understanding, I get so much information, and start to understand in ways I hadn't thought were possible, it's like cleaning very dirty glasses, it's amazing what you can see when you do. Externalising conversations are really good things.*

TIM: *That makes me a little curious. Has this got anything to do with what Dale now believes is true about himself? Or have you reclaimed what you already know about yourself, if that makes sense?*

Positioning yourself in ways   45

DALE: *Yes absolutely, it is reclaiming what I know is truth about myself, it's definitely part of the process of reclaiming who I am now.*

TIM: *What does this imply?*

DALE: *I have found in the past reclaiming who I am has been too hard for me to work out. Because, of the many, many violent sexual acts from Ridsdale which happened so long ago. I have had great difficulty facing my truth … . I can't reclaim who I was before the abuse, but looking back has allowed me to see just how powerful my dad's Christian example and narrative was, how he lived, cared for, supported and loved us, my story is very much like dads, being like my dad is something I aspire too. It's who I am. Thank you Tim so much because it is the first time I have thought about this in depth, and in our conversations you opened that possibility up for me. Wanting to be like my dad. The things my dad used to do for others, and now realising I am living that now is remarkable. The feet of the swan will never stop moving but the water is getting clearer and I can see, understand, look forward and reach out with unconditional love in a way that I never thought I could or would … I am living that now. Thank you.*

At the end of some of Dale's responses, I used an asterisk to indicate potential further conversations. I hoped these follow-up questions would further thicken Dale's new identity conclusions and promote the possibility for Dale to explore his 'acts of resistance' from being positioned in particular dominant discourses (Yuen 2007).

As a consequence of the interviews, which deconstructed shame within dominant societal discourses and further thickened Dale's reclaiming of his integrity, it was now possible to explore Dale's stance with significant others, who aligned with Dale's preferred stories of self. My intention was for these connections with significant others to provide support for the preferred actions Dale wished to take into the future (Carey and Russell 2002). Michael White (2005) refers to the idea that people's identities are shaped by what can be referred to as a 'club of life', and that there are members to our club of life who have had particular parts to play in how we have come to experience ourselves. Using the 'club of life' metaphor with Dale made it possible for him to recount significant people in his life whom he had actively engaged with and who passed on their special knowledges to him – for instance, people who showed compassion and positively contributed to others after the sexual violence. My intention was to support Dale in realising that he was joined with his father (now passed away) in this club – through how Dale had reflected on his life – which further strengthened their connection with each other. We were able to explore these reclaimed knowledges of self that he learnt from his father – who had also experienced sexual violence – which Dale had mentioned previously in our counselling consultations. These re-membering conversations spanned over two sessions.

Initially, we explored Dale's ability 'to see deeper than skin deep' when associating with other people, as a response to the sexual violence he experienced as a child – whether that was by interacting with a passer-by on the street or chatting to a family member around the dinner table. At this point, it was crucial to join these experiences of Dale's with the memories he had of his father and his contribution to Dale's 'alternative account of how he had chosen to live his life'. Following on from these conversations, Dale shared how he wanted to positively contribute to others who have

46   *Positioning yourself in ways*

experienced the similar effects of shame from their experience of sexual violence. It was also important to join these intentions of Dale's with the memory of his father – for instance, connecting how Dale's father had impacted other people's lives positively with Dale's desire to support people who had also experienced sexual violence.

Part one – remembering dad and his influence on Dale's ability 'to see deeper than skin deep'

TIM: *Is there someone in your life that could remind you of your own history of dealing with loss or grief? I know you have mentioned your father, in previous conversations.*

DALE: *Dad is there, Mum is definitely there too.*

TIM: *In what ways?*

DALE: *Mum lost both her parents when she was young … she's a fighter too. Mum struggled with her body image but always fought her way through that self-image, to reach out and help others. Mum and Dad were fairly poor when we were kids; Mum was always able to get a meal out of nothing … always helped other people. She gave other kids something to eat even though we had nothing … she really showed you what it was to give. Mum and Dad backed each other in the way they gave of themselves to help others, and Mum has coped very well since losing Dad.*

TIM: *Wow … what an impact she had. Is it okay if we go back to your dad, and last time when you mentioned him in reference to the swan on the water and madly paddling under the water while appearing calm on the surface?*

DALE: [nodding head] *Dad seemed to do it most of the time. He was a farmer most of his life … he always got through the hard times, somehow … he probably relied on us to help him at times. Being let down by farming neighbours and relatives – I didn't like witnessing Dad go through this… . Dad was heartbroken if a cow died giving birth … he would be out all night with the cow … I saw him sob once having to get the vet to come out and shoot the heifer … he was a very compassionate man. He had a real heart for the land, the animals; and he loved us very much too – even through the tough times, and I saw him reach out lots of times to care for those around him and in the community.*

TIM: *What does this say about what you believe your life to be? Would he be surprised to hear this?*

DALE: *I don't think my dad would be surprised to hear me talk about this; he was a great influence in our lives, he taught us to have good morals, to care and support others through difficult times.*

TIM: *How did your dad carry himself after the sexual violence?*

DALE: *For me, looking back now, knowing the way dad lived and carried himself after his cousin raped him, and threatened to shoot Dad if he told anyone. Dad carried on with life and still put up with his cousin … working with him … tolerating him. I know he didn't like him but that threat to kill Dad was always there so I guess Dad had to love his cousin the best he could … I don't know how Dad did that. My dad was a very strong, compassionate, caring and loving man … an amazing man …*

TIM: *Tell me more, from remembering this …*

DALE: *Dad was an example and showed us how to live life. I need to do the same … I haven't done it really well probably … integrity kicking in now … I need to …work at getting answers. I have the example of my father and mother, what they coped through … why should I be any different?*

Positioning yourself in ways   47

TIM: *What's suggesting that you are any different?*

DALE: *I think that is* [my] *negative thought process. It comes from all the words spoken over me by Ridsdale … as well as the abuse … the name-calling most of my life after the abuse from kids and adults. All that takes a lot to deal with …*

TIM: *What's your belief in life now?*

DALE: *There is that* [internal] *fight that those people who called me names knew more than I did … they witnessed some of those things* [the abuse]; *they were verbalising what they saw. Which was true … .*

TIM: *True about what?*

DALE: *I was involved in what they may have been involved in… .And they coped in their own way by calling me names. That is a revelation … I see that now – everyone comes from somewhere … those same hurts, – shame, guilt, pain, fear…*

TIM: *You mean the 'deeper than skin deep?'*

DALE: *Definitely – and unfortunately it comes out in words sometimes, which you can't take away.*

TIM: *What does this say about what you are trying to do with your life? How do you continue to contribute to their living memory?*

DALE: *Now?*

TIM: *Yeah.*

DALE: *I'd love it to all go away, that can't happen, so I'm facing the truth. Tim, you have enabled me to continue to contribute to Dad's living memory by awakening me through these externalising and scaffolding conversations to reflect on how I was brought up and to reflect on the great Christian morals, strengths and the loving examples of my parents… giving me the skills to start living my life, through their great example.*

TIM: *How do you do that now?*

DALE: *Integrity is a big part of that striving … it's the driving force to reflect on those things that I have learnt through watching my parents and trying to be better … understanding that everyone usually comes to a place of hurt, particularly when they are not very nice.*

TIM: *Are you contributing to your dad's living memory now?*

DALE: *I want to live life to the best of my ability … try and do the right things and put others before myself … do the best I can in what I have learnt from life and my parents.*

TIM: *Are there any practical ways of how you can / are doing this?*

DALE: *It is very easy to judge … so I think, be careful in what you say … look deeply into other people's situations and don't judge ever …*

TIM: *Have there been any recent times?*

DALE: *I try to pull people up actually … Mum said something negative about the Japanese in the car on the way home … after being treated appallingly by an Asian dentist…*

TIM: *Your dad obviously struggled coping with the Japanese after the war?*

DALE: *Dad hated them … but he did forgive them.* [Mum said:] *'All the Japanese in the war were nasty people'. I said: 'Mum, you can't say that; you can't say ALL … maybe some of them … just like us …. some of us are nice … some of us aren't'.*

TIM: *And Mum's response?*

DALE: *She knew … she knew what she said. 'Okay, I understand that' were her words. You can't generalise with things like that Mum!*

TIM: *And your dad, if he was in the car?*

48   *Positioning yourself in ways*

DALE: *Probably would have responded in the same way. I tried to understand my dad's experiences – in New Guinea, the Japanese were cruel to the Fuzzy Wuzzies they would get them to unload boats and carry heavy artillery along the beach, then the Japs would shoot them dead after they had finished with them. Dad said the Fuzzy Wuzzies were amazing – he loved them, he was heartbroken to see them treated with such hatred.*

TIM: *What does sharing this message of being able to go 'deeper than skin deep' with people mean to you? What would your dad be saying, if he were in the room today?*

DALE: *It's important to understand people... . I believe that you have to go 'deeper than skin'. You take the time to get to know someone ... there is such rich blessing from that. You usually find that there is someone different inside that skin ...*

TIM: *What would your dad be saying if he was hearing this?*

DALE: *He'd probably be amazed at what I'd learnt from him. Dad's father died when Dad was young so Dad didn't really have an example to follow. Dad said his father was a sick man and not very loving ... he didn't have a really good role model. So for him to be a really good father ... he had to teach himself ... learnt as he went ...and he did a great job.*

TIM: *Stopping that cycle?*

DALE: *He'd be very emotional.*

TIM: *In what way?*

DALE: *It would be an awakening for him ... in a positive sense. He'd be sobbing – in joy, probably a bit of both – joy in knowing what he had achieved through what I shared and hurt in realising how hard it all was... . He died before I had a chance to tell him my story; I hadn't come to terms with the abuse myself when he died. Dad never told me directly about his cousin abusing him. I found out through a family member.*

TIM: *What would it show?*

DALE: *That he fought hard and won ...*

TIM: *Can you see parallels with your own life?*

DALE: *[I did] just then ... yeah.*

TIM: *What's this making possible for you now?*

DALE: *I can do it too ... I am doing it.*

TIM: *What have you found useful today and is there anything that you will take away?*

DALE: *It was really good ... it was all good ... I will take away all of it. I think it is really good to reflect on what examples I have had from my parents and my life experiences ... and to share that stuff, everyone who has experienced sexual abuse probably has these same thoughts and fears* [early on in the session].

TIM: *So the alternative account of Dale, where does that sit now?*

DALE: *You mean not the old? I am getting better at dealing with the negatives and looking forward positively with integrity... . I know my experiences of violent sexual abuse will never go away but what I have gained from great counselling is I can live with the truth, and I can help others to do the same and to break their silence and live, love and never judge. Putting yourself into the people and things that matter.*

TIM: *How can you continue to do this?*

DALE: *Keep organising a wedding* [said with a smile, referring to his daughter's upcoming wedding].

Positioning yourself in ways   49

Part two – remembering dad's influence on Dale's desire to contribute to others

TIM: *What will it mean for others to hear about part of your story of 'walking alongside' – the effects of sexual violence – and how you have responded … ?*

DALE: *The people who have experienced similar things will be more open* [to hearing my story] *… I'm very aware* [now]*… to look for signs.*

TIM: *What signs do you see?*

DALE: *To cope with it … I feel that resistance, of being rejected, to open up … I need to listen … read them … look deeper than skin… . Last weekend, I was talking to a relative … . His mother had told him about the sexual abuse I had experienced. I shared more about my story to him, which opened the way for him to share more openly, I shared my thoughts about that… . He then told me he loved me, it was quite emotional. I guess I was promoting – and opening – a way for him, allowing him to … open up about his story.*

TIM: *What did you provide?*

DALE: *The right environment, the opening up and honesty in the conversation, releasing the balloon of shame, hurt, guilt … well, the beginning of it.*

TIM: *What does it mean, for you, to talk about challenging the dominant discourses/ thoughts of around what it is to be a man? Who taught you this?*

DALE: *I have struggled to have friendships with other males after my experiences of sexual abuse – for example, even with coping to book and take my car in for a service … dealing with ocker male environments is a real problem for me. I was able to share with my relative … challenging my distrust of people … that's a good thing … exposing that vulnerability of Dale's. Allowing myself to share … not worrying about the consequences of being vulnerable… I can't. I don't care what they think … I AM MALE.*

TIM: *What does this say about you not accepting certain ways of being?*

DALE: *Besides my Dad, I had no other* [positive] *role models. Dad wanted me to be a sports person. I rebelled against that. He made me go to football training, for three seasons; I did the bare minimum. Dad didn't know about the terrible bullying I was enduring. When I did get picked on team, I went and hid in the cubby in the forest until the game was over. It took guts to go against my father's wishes. I was a bit rebellious … STICKING UP FOR MYSELF … taught by the abuse.*

TIM: *How will this contribute to the protest against what it means to be a man?*

DALE: *You can't say I'm not a man … I guess you learn along the way. I have learnt from my father not to push my kids into anything* [they don't want to do]. *You need to allow the gentle side of being a male to come out … it is a strength being gentle … protects, doesn't it? Some younger males these days appear to be more gentle … not sure if society knows what it means to be a man.*

TIM: *What does this say about what you are trying to do with your life?*

DALE: *Trying to fix it … life's not easy …*

TIM: *In what way?*

DALE: *I just don't like how narrow people are … making judgements on others. Words can be such horrible things … they don't go away. It'd be really good to say to people, just think about what you are going to say before you say it.*

TIM: *What does this suggest about what you believe your life should be?*

DALE: *Making it possible to see deeper than skin deep, is it a spiritual gift? Not sure. I can see that I am a male that is strong, gentle and I love to help others … I do … I have for a long time. I think it gives me the ability to … to win the race … I mean it takes a lot of fight and guts to get through this.*

50 *Positioning yourself in ways*

TIM: *What does thinking about winning the race make possible for Dale?*

DALE: *It would be great not to think about the sexual abuse anymore … not let it dominate my life. Having a day without it would be great, but it's not like that – it doesn't go away, So, if I can help someone who has experienced sexual abuse, that will always mean I'm winning the race. There is a reason for everything …*

TIM: *Who else that you know of hasn't accepted certain ways of living? Or is there a figure who took risks to make a life of their own?*

DALE: *Jesus. He will be there even in the tough times … it helps give peace to Dale … I know what Jesus did … He gave his life … went through pain for us …*

TIM: *What does this say about what Jesus stood for?*

DALE: *He wasn't accepting evil … I wouldn't be here today if I didn't have that knowledge. I do want to face it now.*

TIM: *Who is Dale now?*

DALE: *I see openness to not judging … everyone sees something differently. You can't make a judgement on people. Something that has put me off going to church is how I see the people making judgements on others; that's something that we as Christians are called not to do, judge others.*

TIM: *What does this say about who you are?*

DALE:

- *Don't like judging people*
- *There is a strength in the gentleness*
- *Don't want anyone to be hurt*
- *Want to make things right*
- *Contribute to others lives in a positive way*
- *Keep being who God created me to be … it is still developing … we are always developing. Jane – a friend of mine – would see who I am … she would say that I am a good listener, a person so reliant on God with prayer, I have an openness.*

TIM *Is there something that was useful today or something you will take away with you?*

DALE *The way I see myself. What sort of person I am … open, rebellious, [a person of] humour.*

Michael White (2002) describes the 'rites of passage' metaphor as offering another frame that can assist us in making meaning that is acknowledging of the movement that we experience in the conversations we have with the people who consult us. At this time, it was important to thicken Dale's new identity conclusion, so together Dale and I decided to write a letter to Shame. The intention of the letter was to promote further unyielding of Dale's rich story development, continuing his migration into reclaiming his integrity. We were committed to freeing Dale from the negative effects that shame had placed on him. Deciding to share this letter with others was significant … what was now being shared were Dale's truths.

Dear Shame,

I am not sure if you are happy with me not wanting you in my life, which I know upsets you. You have influenced me in such a strong way in the past and mostly you are still there … maybe I will never totally get rid of you.

Positioning yourself in ways   51

Your practices of keeping me silent for forty years allowed me to get on with my life. This was an effect I never thought was positive, until recently. But it did make me think twice about not knowing who I am.

Your tricks of self-doubt got in the way of me trusting people; you kept that lie alive because I didn't believe anyone would believe my story of sexual abuse. I know when you creep your way back into my life because sadness, anger, fear, tears, and so much emotion comes back. Now I am seeing your tricks and the effects – you are broken, Shame, and I know I can break through your power.

I have discovered who I am, letting Integrity step into the room more now. Even though the physical effects are still there and the nightmares keep you alive in my life, Integrity has given me hope that you can now be silenced. 'I don't give a shit what you think anymore'.

Well Shame … you have taught me a lot about what it means to be me, and the strength of you in my life has been a direct correlation to the strength of what I value and hold onto. I can see this now, which minimises your influence on me.

If my integrity wasn't so strong, I don't think your influence would have been so overpowering. Let me explain: Shame, you made me blame myself for the sexual abuse I experienced all those years ago. I was brought up to believe in people and to respect adults who were in a position of authority, trusted to influence my life. You have reminded me of what I stand for.

Now it is Integrity that gets me thinking … hahaha. I now remember who I am and what I have taught my family and my children. I am reminded of my daughter and a story of her determination to speak up, which I am sure she got from me. Sharing this story makes me laugh and gets me thinking about when I first made a stand against you. But for now I will share about my daughter. I know Tim, who I see [and 'walk alongside'], was impacted by this story. My daughter was only four at the time and I was washing her hair in the bath. After I got soap in her eyes, she said to me, 'if this happens again, I am leaving.' Well … it wasn't long before she leapt out of the bath, grabbed her case and left through the front door. By the time I got to her, she was halfway down the street. Making a stand is important for her and now that she is an adult, ready to get married, I am sure she will make her voice known in that relationship. You can't silence me anymore, Shame, and making a stand is very important to me, which has influenced my daughter. Standing up for what's right together.

I am now more in control of my relationship with you, Shame. I don't have to wear that hat anymore and telling the truth is important to me. I am not sure if I can thank you for what you brought into my life, but you have allowed me to think about the effects that you have had on me differently now and how Integrity is now putting a silence on you.

Through my knowledge of being a victim/survivor of sexual abuse/violence, I now know that truth kept in silence was controlled by you, Shame, and the lie that that held in my life is that the truth is shameful. So I believe that speaking or sharing these truths is a great start to breaking through that falsehood of shame. Because sharing the truth starts the process to freedom, freedom from you, Shame … ,

52   *Positioning yourself in ways*

Shame, you have been overpowering; Shame, it was you who kept me silent; Shame, you pulled me down and controlled me; Shame, you stopped me from handling the truth. The Bible says in John 8:32, the truth will set you free … that's the truth. Shame, you're a liar… .

Thank you, Tim for allowing me to speak directly to Shame; you have been instrumental in making me aware of what Shame has caused in me for forty-odd years. The thing is with me … I knew the truth and that it would set me free, but Shame, you had your way in me and overpowered the truth and caused me to be silenced. Causing me to feel too shameful, that the sexual abuse was my fault … the sexual response of my body too shameful … which brings in fear, and then you, Shame, become a powerful force always pressing me down. Shame, you and fear hold hands; I never want to be under that duo again. Finally, speaking this out loud to you, Tim, and us writing this letter, I believe is a great start to freedom and moving out from under the darkness of shame and fear into the promised light of finally sharing the truth. It is a process, but the truth does set you free. Shame, I've worked you out.

With every blessing, Dale

After the letter to Shame was written, I read it back to Dale, which then prompted a realisation from him that sharing the truth in this way brought a sense of 'freedom in uncovering the truth and not denying the fact that I was there'. As an intervention, therapeutic letters may arouse us gently, boldly and ethically to uphold the integrity of relationships in counselling through the durable tradition of the written word. Therapeutic letters (Frayling 2010):

- challenge conventional notions of what's boundaried, within the therapeutic context
- represent a relationally responsive practice
- provide educational methods of reflecting with the people we consult.

At this time, conversations centred on Dale's local meanings gained from his upbringing, where he was brought up to respect people and how he now influences his own family and his children in a positive way. Focusing on what motivates Dale to stand up for what he believes in when sharing the truth, he was able to share that, 'I wouldn't have thought like this in the past … there was a purpose to it [referencing his experiences of sexual violence] … all those things brought me to where I am today'. These conversations enabled an *acceptance* from Dale, and even though this new sharing was painful for him, there was power in his acknowledgment that the sexual violence did happen and it was the truth.

Michael White (2004) invites therapists and psychologists to consider 'folk psychology' to explore 'the local meanings and ways of understanding life that people bring' to the counselling room, and David Denborough (2008) introduces the idea of reinvigorating folk culture as a response to trauma. The challenge within any organisation is how we can promote the sharing of local meanings and ways of understanding life that people bring that has the potential to provide rich meaning, comfort, celebration and solace.

Positioning yourself in ways   53

**

> Is this a useful consideration in your own practice? Have there been ways that you have been able to provide a space of collective influence in your own work setting?

**

Though it is important to consider bringing the therapeutic conversations into the public sphere, an ongoing consideration in our practice is the equal importance of being attentive to the individual's experience, which requires ongoing measuring, if we are to provide an environment that is safe and encouraging to share beyond the four walls of counselling. There are many ways that collective action can be made possible that gives consideration to this, such as exchange of emails between clients that is filtered through the practitioner, having the client respond to a letter that was published in a book where that person had written about similar experiences. Therefore, the question begs to be asked: How are we able to work with the individual in carrying their voice into a space of collective influence without pushing our own agenda? Especially when they are feeling that they are not ready to bring their voice into the open? (Denborough 2008).

Notes

1 Exploring Dale's account of the truth, remembering people close to him who see him as a person who does know the truth.
2 Exploring an alternate story, an exception to the problem story when shame isn't around.

8 Wrestling through shame and sharing stories of resistance

Key points to consider:

- <u>Shoring up the client's reclaimed knowledge</u>: *Allowing space for client's to share their own experiences of trauma with other people.*

During the next phase in my walk with Dale, I was challenged to question the limitations of dominant one-on-one counselling approaches that promote the idea that the client can only share their problematic experiences with the counsellor and should remain private. Even though this approach promotes boundaries and safety, there are so many other stories about how people experience relief and the shaking off of shame. Furthermore, when stories are shared and connections are made with others who have experienced similar trauma, opportunities are presented for the person to further thicken up new identity conclusions that wouldn't have been possible in traditional approaches to counselling (Handsacker 2012). In addition, I came to the conclusion that if clients are able to share stories together, the opportunity presents for the person to shore up their reclaimed knowledge – knowledge that was gained from the skills and abilities they utilised when responding to the sexual violence, or any acts of oppression for that matter. Therefore, is the apprehension to allow space for people to *share* their own experiences of trauma with other people who have experienced something similar – rather than only in an individualistic counselling approach – about managing our own risk as professionals?

> Sharing the stories in this way becomes a political act by publicly putting the spotlight on the one who has subjected the other to sexual harm and by providing an opportunity for all of us to clearly expose the discourses that keep these acts secret.
>
> (Davidson, personal communication 2015)

Thus, it is useful to consider that many of the people that we consult with have little opportunity to feel as if they are making a contribution to the lives of others, which arguably is compounded by the individualistic nature of traditional counselling approaches. The client may feel despair and anguish that they struggle to get their own life together, let alone be able to offer something to someone else. The

DOI: 10.4324/9781003256816-9

difficulties that people are facing, however, will not be theirs alone and their experiences of harm and how they have responded to the hurt can offer a contribution to others in similar or related situations (Handsacker 2012).

Significantly, the experience of inputting into the lives of others can be the catalyst to reduce the effects (or transform the nature) of the suffering in the person's life. With Dale, his sharing brought a sense that his suffering has not been for nothing, which ignited a sense of possibility that swelled over to other aspects of his life (Denborough 2008).

Towards the end of Dale's therapeutic journey, we were motivated to raise awareness around the influence of shame in sexual abuse when victims are silenced. Above all, we were committed to stopping the prevalence of sexual abuse and the stigma surrounding talking about it publicly. What was being made possible by Dale taking action to share his story, and the two of us sharing information about our work together, is that we were not only restoring Dale's preferred way of being, but our conversations were invigorated by our being able to contribute to a social movement supporting other people who have had similar experiences. The idea of 'the need to adopt antiviolence strategies that are mindful of the larger structures of violence that shape the world in which we live' (Handsacker 2012) is a central consideration in our practice when working with people's experiences of oppression. I have had many conversations with clients around exposing the truth regarding power relations in sexual violence, and how sharing their story will hopefully assist others in reclaiming their lives by contributing to a deeper understanding of shame. This development is quite significant, given the journey Dale and I are now on. Specifically, we hope that the conversation we have with people has the capacity to restore the person's sense of personal agency, enabling them to make a contribution in challenging broader social issues related to what influences shame – for instance, dominant masculinity. This has been a very important step in deconstructing the power that was given to shame in silencing Dale's values and beliefs.

Following on from our newfound intentions, we decided to respond to a story in David Denborough's book *Collective Narrative Practice* (2008) – in particular a letter from Paul, who Denborough interviewed while Paul was in prison. Paul had experienced sexual abuse as a child. Together Dale and I set about writing a response to Paul's letter, which has been included here (below). Up to this point, Dale and I had been 'walking alongside' each other for approximately thirty sessions. Dale and I were now beginning to locate Dale's experiences, as Denborough (2008) described, as:

- representing a social issue
- joining in a collective endeavour in addressing the social issue through their local knowledges from what they experienced
- speaking to someone who has had similar experiences and identifying ways for co-contributing to each other's lives.

Significantly, the letter Dale wrote to Paul promoted further unyielding of his rich story development, continuing his migration into not being silenced anymore and speaking the truths of his experiences. Also I was promoting a collective narrative practice – an emerging field in narrative therapy described in Denborough's

56   *Wrestling through shame*

book – through Dale responding to an adult male in prison who had also experienced sexual violence.

Dear Paul,

My name is Dale, and I thank you for being so open in sharing your personal story and struggles, which I found very moving as I read your letter. I understand how you are feeling and as you would know, it is not easy to share your story of sexual abuse at any time, no matter where you are. Shame is a powerful, unpleasant self-conscious emotion which causes a negative evaluation of self and brings about withdrawal and silence. It has taken me forty-two years to start talking about my story of traumatic child sexual abuse by a Catholic priest over a period of twenty-eight months 1973–1975.

Thank you for writing your letter sharing your lived experiences and what you have shared of your personal journey to try and make sense of the silence, which is of great encouragement to other survivors. My abuser told me he loved me, the abuse was our secret and I was never to tell anyone or I would be punished. Every time I was sexually abused I pushed it into the depths of my being, a place where I thought it was hidden, so, I shut it away and never told a soul.

I am now speaking about my experiences after having great counselling, but I am not saying this is not difficult, painful, emotional or re-traumatising because it definitely is all those things. My counsellor Tim has given me the understanding and the ability to reignite my integrity and Christian values of knowing right from wrong; these strengths evoked the truth to me – that the abuse was not my fault and together we have worked out shame's undermining effects. Now I have a deeper understanding of the way shame works, I can push through shame's power with integrity, which has broken the silence.

Paul, you have shared something very similar in your letter – 'It's best to just talk about your experiences of child sexual abuse in a matter-of-fact way'. That's great advice, because it's as you say, much harder not to talk about it, and you express how important it's been for you not to worry about what the other person thinks, but it is necessary to trust the person you share your story with. Also, facing the emotion and re-traumatising – it's important to let the emotion happen; we block out so much of our stories, but taking the chance to experience it again means we can have a relationship with our own life, our past, that little kid. What incredible advice.

The joining of stories is a fantastic way to break the silence with someone who understands, who has been through similar circumstances. Sharing the truth of our stories is such an important start to helping each other start to live again; it's so freeing when someone else actually knows the truth of your story, breaking through the shame, pain and fear, and the guilt of being squashed or judged in the past.

Paul, you talk about wanting to fix your life. I hope and pray that as you talk about your story and share it with others, breaking the silence, that you and

Wrestling through shame   57

those you share with will find a deeper understanding of shame, bringing you a freedom that will indeed fix your life.

Thank you so much for sharing.

Dale

After the letter to Paul was written Dale shared:

> ... truth kept in silence is controlled by shame and the lie that holds is that the truth is shameful. So I believe that speaking or the sharing of these truths is a great start to breaking through that falsehood of shame. Because sharing the truth starts the process to freedom, freedom from shame... . Shame is over-powering, shame keeps you silent ... shame pulls you down and controls ... shame also stops you from handling the truth ...
>
> Finally, speaking this out loud to you and I believe for myself and others it is a great start to freedom and moving out from under the darkness of shame and fear into the promised light of finally sharing the truth. It is a process, but the truth does set you free.

Dale was developing a deeper understanding of shame and the power it once had over his life. What had been made possible with Dale, when taking action in the form of a letter, was that he had heard a story of hope, from another child who had also experienced sexual abuse. It was Dale's and Paul's knowledge that enabled them to speak the truth about their experiences of sexual abuse, thus lessening the effects of shame in both their lives.

Through conversations that enable people to share skills, lives can become joined through a shared sense of values, beliefs, purpose and commitment. As a practitioner, introducing these ideas requires a fine balance in responding to what is in front of you in a careful and thoughtful way; and also, in finding timely and appropriate ways to speak about the person's experiences of being validated, and of collaboration and connection. This needs to be done without 'side-racking' from the person's preferences of conversation (Handsacker 2012). This means that there are days when the thoughts of the person seeing us need prioritising, and there are days when we need to hold the conversation around the person's experiences – for instance, fear, shame and safety. It is important that the exchange doesn't become about what we are 'centring' – that is, becoming focused on our own agenda. It needs to be timely, considered and have resonance for both people. Choosing the right time in the session for these conversations takes careful consideration of safety in the room, without influencing the conversation in a way that might reignite the powerlessness the person felt when they initially presented for support.

★★

How do you catch yourself out when a conversation becomes focused on your own agenda?

58 *Wrestling through shame*

★★

Now that Dale was no longer being silenced, I asked him this question: 'What do the moments of freedom from shame look like? And how can you contribute to social movement that breaks the silence of childhood sexual abuse?' It had taken thirty-five sessions to get to this point. Dale responded with the following letter, promoting freedom in how he now wishes to share his truth and contribute to others who have had similar experiences.

Tim,

I have been thinking and chewing through these questions for a while now – what does freedom from shame look like? And how can Dale contribute to social movement … the social issue of child sexual abuse?

Shame had a way of holding me in a place of oppression; it has held me in a place of not coping with the truth … which strangely allowed me to live in a depressive state for forty-odd years, in complete denial of the sexual abuse and violence. So shame also underpinned me by me taking on and believing I deserved the verbal and physical abuse – also by dreams and protective repetitive behaviour. Shame took away my childhood, shame also helped me in a strange way … because the truth was too shameful and painful. I buried it which allowed me to live my life, get married and have a beautiful family. Now I have worked shame out. Shame made me play the self-blame game – it looks like when shame doesn't have control … truth holds the key – shame has no place in the truth … I can talk about my experience of sexual abuse and shame is not in the room … in fact, nowhere to be found. But I am finding that there is no word to describe how painful the truth is – strangely, shame has protected me from this … it has been tough, excruciatingly painful … after forty years, to face the truth of child sexual abuse, now at age fifty-two. Freedom from shame looks like … a caged bird out of a dark dungeon, placed on the edge of a cliff … not knowing how to fly. The scars are deep, they weep blood, the scars look like a bird that's been locked in a dark dungeon and every time I was sexually abused, parts of my wings rotted away. As I sort through memories, I look hard to find the light … pre sexual abuse … could I fly then? I had hardly been let out of the nest. But I must learn how to fly … can I take the risk on this cliff? The pain is incredibly real. I have just experienced a complete psychological assessment – there are no words to describe what that was like. I was only allowed to speak when answering a question. In two hours, I had to speak about a time pre sexual abuse … to every detail of the sexual abuse, the effects on me and how I coped … also how I am coping today. At times I struggled to verbalise what was inside of me. I didn't tell her everything – this has had a horrific effect on me mentally. I am not coping with life … that experience of frightening accusations and judgements heaved me back into the dark, damp stench of the dungeon, almost like I have lost the fight. I need help to be built up, I don't like it in here. I feel very exposed, this

Wrestling through shame   59

is not shame … this is the truth. I had hoped it would set me free and give me the will to fly again, now I understand shame.

I want to fly again and I want to help others who have experienced child sexual abuse to fly again too … but I need to learn how to do that again. As hard as the psychological assessment was, it was like being in a boxing ring and smacking me across the face with every truth that came out of me. It was horrific, but it also exposed me to facing the truth head on, and I had not done that before … reliving everything in a short period of time … also the realisation that this is me. It revealed just how fucked my life is. As difficult as this is, it makes me believe that life can't get any worse, and putting all that Tim and I have worked at aside … facing the truth and surviving through it has been the biggest challenge.

The psychological assessment Dale is referring to here was a clinical assessment he was subjected to prior to his Royal Commission involvement. Taking part in the Commission was part of actioning his commitment to not being silenced anymore. After the assessment, he was able to share with me the experience of 'powerlessness' that he felt while being assessed, and how these feelings were linked back to his experience of childhood sexual violence. Furthermore, Dale was able to deconstruct his own experiences regarding how he continues to not be silenced. He was now able to talk about these experiences in ways that strengthened his purpose and commitment to sharing the truth.

TIM: *So… tell me more about that experience of being heaved back into the dark deep stench* [using Dale's previously used words]. *What was that about?*

DALE: *I wasn't able to prepare; it was cold and clinical. I had to answer her questions and I was told 'not now' – we will get to that later.*

TIM: *If you were to name the effects of that 'being heaved back into the dark stench', is there a name that resonates for you?*

DALE: *I didn't want to be there anymore.*

TIM: *I get the sense that there wasn't any containment for you in what was being asked? These are my words, of course. You had no control and the power was with the doctor. Would that be right?*

DALE: *With what happened* [the sexual abuse], *they had the power over me and with the doctor – this links back to the control from Ridsdale … every day I uncover myself from this shit.*

TIM: *Are there any similarities between what you experienced with the doctor and your experiences of sexual abuse?*

DALE: *Yeah … I think so… I was still living it. Seeing the doctor put me back in a place of heaviness.*

TIM: *What's that about?*

DALE: *The frustration … you can't understand it if you haven't lived it … every day I uncover from the shit and the darkness.*

TIM: *Tell me more about the shit and the darkness?*

60 *Wrestling through shame*

DALE: *It's like being covered in a pile of shit … these experiences, like with the doctor… a word that someone says … a flashback … I'm back in the hole … under the shit again … because it momentarily takes you back* [to the experiences of sexual abuse].

TIM: *What is being made possible knowing that it is momentarily?*

DALE: *I'm learning to live with it… deal with it.*

TIM: *Tell me more?*

DALE: *I've come to the conclusion, I have to… the challenge is to live with it… it's like a rollercoaster.*

TIM: *You talked about expectations earlier… is it more than that? What do you expect?*

DALE: *I didn't want to be here anymore* [after the doctor's visit]*… it was my family's expectations … my children acknowledging me, accepting me, their appreciation of, I'm always there for them. Their expectations come out of their love for me. Living for others is important to me.*

TIM: *What has been useful about today?*

DALE: *Getting this stuff out … it makes sense. The reason I'm still here is because there are people here that love me… I need those things to get out of the hole* [of powerlessness].

TIM: *So, these expectations … can I ask you, where is this located in relation to the effects of shame?*

DALE: *I'm confused about that.*

Up to this point, there had been much care and attention paid to externalising the effects of shame, therefore enabling the following questions to be asked in a follow-up session. Dale's definition of self was no longer being totalised by his experiences of sexual abuse.

TIM: *Where does Dale sit now, with the confusion around shame – for instance, the good and bad effects, the in-between.*

DALE: *I believed shame had been dealt with, and I believe that shame protected me from facing the truth which allowed me to live my life… . I believe it was not my shame it was his, Ridsdale's shame that I carried … and his shame that protected me. Now his shame is gone, I feel like that crumpled, hurt piece of paper, exposed to the truth – SEXUAL ABUSE – and the memories of that don't go away, they linger, hovering under the surface of who I am. This is life right now. Some days I don't handle it very well; some days I don't want to be here anymore; and some days I feel fine.*

TIM: *Living with sitting on top of the pile of shit and the momentary times of experienced powerlessness – what does this look like? What is the view like? What are your intentions of sitting on top of the shit?*

DALE: *It's like not having the strength to get up out of bed and face another day with extreme tiredness. The view is knowing whatever you do firstly, is struggling to overcome those feelings – of facing the day, but knowing I have to pull the strength to do it from somewhere. My faith is very helpful … pray myself into the shower … finding the strength to get out of the shower … I don't want to … but I do – dry myself, get dressed. Sitting on top of the shit pile is better than being covered in it; it takes a lot to stay there but I can't move on right now because I'm afraid any minute now I could fall back in the shit … with court proceedings … Royal Commission starting again soon, going over my personal story again. My intention of sitting on top of the shit pile is … that I feel I am*

Wrestling through shame 61

in control a bit more. It feels like I can have a future … I can feel the love of my family … and that gives me the strength and knowledge that I have to fight this …

TIM: *What does it look like to live on the edge of the shit? Is there freedom in that? What does the fear look like? And its effects?*

DALE: *It's lighter up here … and the heaviness is not constant – it comes and goes. Oh yes, I can breathe up here … that in a sense is freedom. I can't look ahead because of the fear that comes with that … it puts me back in the hole. I have to live in the moment* [referenced later]. *Fear comes when I see the pain and tears in my mum's eyes, my siblings, and my wife and children … the stress and fear they feel because they love me and hate what I am going through. I fear because I am causing this in them … and I can't do anything about that … I want to help them but … I make it worse.*

At this point, Dale and I had been 'walking alongside' each other for thirty-six sessions. Dale was able to locate his understanding of shame through his own history of experiences and learnings of right and wrong – implying he had a long-held knowledge of his own integrity. Dale was then invited to consider the idea of deconstructing these ideas in the form of a tree.

9 Discerning shame and speaking the truth with integrity

Dale's Tree of Life

Key points to consider

- <u>Increasing mastery over the problem</u>: *Inviting the client to exercise personal agency over the problem, while making visible their values.*
- <u>Using a tree as a metaphor for life</u>: *Finding a way of explaining or making meaning of events in our lives forms the plot of our story.*

The next phase in my walk with Dale involved the adaptation of the 'Tree of Life' metaphor, exploring Dale's history of knowing right from wrong while standing up for justice. The Tree of Life is a collective narrative approach developed by Ncazelo Ncube and David Denborough (2008) in response to children's trauma. This metaphor was a useful way to deconstruct Dale's problematic stories around shame, which could then be spoken about in ways that strengthened Dale's relationships with his own history, culture and the significant people in his life. Together we aimed to bring to light Dale's own skills and knowledges to provide Dale with an increased connectedness to his family, values and cultural heritage. We completed the Tree of Life activity over nine sessions.

Using a tree chosen by Dale that was representative of his journey with shame (see Appendix G), Dale wrote key words along the parts of the tree based on a series of questions (see Appendix F). My role was to support Dale in distancing himself from the known and familiar that was being reproduced in his relationships with shame. I provided incremental questions that supported Dale to move to a place where it was possible for him to recognise and act on his integrity. This promoted distance from and an increased mastery over his problems, which then invited Dale to gradually exercise personal agency over the shame he was struggling with and make visible the integrity he had already begun to find, which was gaining strength through our conversation (Hayward 2006).

The stories we tell about our lives are formed through linking certain events together in a particular sequence across a time period. Finding a way of explaining or making meaning of these events forms the plot of the story. We always give meaning to our experiences as we live our lives. As Morgan (2000, p.5) says: 'A narrative is like a thread that weaves the events together, forming a story', and the way we develop these stories is established by how we have linked particular events

DOI: 10.4324/9781003256816-10

Discerning shame and speaking the truth 63

together in a sequence and by the meaning we ascribe to them. When we move from one stage of life to another, it can make all the difference if we use the expertise we developed in the first stage to face the difficult situations of the next. For instance, all that we learnt in autumn can assist us to deal with winter. All that we learnt during winter can help us throughout spring. And all that we learnt in spring can provide comfort during summer. Only when there is this sense of continuity can we look forward to life. And as the seasons cycle, we can then remember what we have passed through, how we have transformed, and how we have remained the same (Abu Rayyan 2009). Following is the conversation exploring Dale's history of making a stand for what's right, moving from the roots of the tree to the flowers on his tree – the legacies Dale wishes to leave behind. I have included excerpts of the questions asked during the activity. Initially, I invited Dale to consider his history of making a stand for what's right represented in the roots.

TIM: *Okay. What is your history of making a stand for what's right – that is, not being silenced. Who taught you that?*

DALE: *Jesus – example … Psalm 139. Mum and Dad's examples of overcoming adversity in their personal, family and farm life, from harsh and hurtful words and actions by farming neighbours and others, death of Mum and Dad's parents at a young age, and Dad being raped by a cousin, surviving – silenced and threatened to be shot if he told anyone. All his life until his death bed and coping with that person nearly every day of his life … Mum daily overcoming problems with her self-image. Mum and Dad always taught us to be there and support one another whenever we could, and we did that. On rare occasions I did stick up for others, like for Mum after a difficult dentist appointment and for myself after a guy took my mowing job. I have also learnt heaps through watching and supporting my children through difficult times.*

We then explored the ground of Dale's tree, which represents 'where you live at present' – some of the activities that you choose to do each day. Dale expressed that what he took away from this session was, 'seeing that I have a solid foundation'. Furthermore, he realised that he would 'learn to live with the sexual abuse'. Significantly, Dale was able to recount how he was currently taking action on this idea and how people close to him were being affected by the fact that he was no longer silenced, particularly his friend Robert.

TIM: *Who grounds you now in being aware of your moral obligations of what's right and wrong?*

DALE: *Definitely Jesus and His Word; also the good solid, supportive, loving parents, siblings and home life, which all gave me a great moral foundation. Also, my wife and children ground me in what's right and wrong. I can now see the truth, thinking about where I came from, that I started life with a solid foundation.*

TIM: *Has there been an example of how you have been able to speak up in uncovering the truth of shame, currently?*

DALE: *For me as a sexual abuse victim, the truth of shame has been revealed – shame covered the truth, causing me to be focused on my part in the sexual act and my body's response to the sexual act. The truth about shame is, it makes you vulnerable to self-blame or to believing because of my body's natural response to a sexual act that there must be something wrong*

64 *Discerning shame and speaking the truth*

with me ... but that's a lie. I have recently been trying to help Robert, my friend, with his journey after sexual abuse and I believe I have been able to help him. This is part of a recent email [he sent me] in reply to trying to help him with the truth of shame.

> *Dear Dale,*
>
> *I did get your emails and your thoughtful text – you give to me the ultimate gift, the belief from one human being to another that my life has mattered ... and the view I have of myself is not necessarily the view of others – you generously give me the self-belief I secretly lack. I'm so very grateful that you have been my true witness, and after all these years, I am no longer alone in the vortex of childhood sexual abuse. I feel strengthened knowing you care about me. I hope that you also feel my love and support in a time of unbearable pain. Do you ever feel alone in your memories of what happened to you? I know that, through the years, I have often been struck down, unable to exist, unable to go forth, unable to respond to the expectations of life, and that is why I feel as though I have often damaged relationships. Lately I've felt so comforted by our conversations and the burden of secrets shared with you has greatly eased my mind. However, I am deeply grieved by what you are going through, your flood of memories and the enormous pain that goes with the recall is what we have in common. It was our destiny that as boys we suffered a similar fate, and forty years on, I'm thankful that I have you beside me, a wise and loving friend who makes me very happy and makes me feel for the first time in my life that I can come home, there is nothing to fear .. Dale, thank you for being such a constant in my life; all the messages and the love has been truly inspiring. I think what you do in friendship is very special – you not only recognise the pain and suffering in others, you then set about mending and healing the broken. You never give up, your desire to love your fellow man is Divine – and I love you back.*
>
> *You Have A Beautiful Soul.*
> *From Your Friend Robert.*

After sharing this letter, Dale then spoke about his friendship with Robert, which spanned over forty-six years. Robert had also experienced sexual abuse, and this sharing between them validated their friendship. Furthermore, in Dale's words, Robert is 'someone who has been through the same thing. And the shared understanding is important – they are struggling still, and we are able to talk about it in a lighthearted way'.

Next it was possible to explore the trunk of the tree, which symbolised what Dale is good at, focusing on the skills and abilities he learnt along the way, in gaining a deeper understanding of shame. The purpose of this was to promote further distancing from the effects of shame.

TIM: *Are you good at looking after people? How did you learn this?*

DALE: *Yes, I am. I learnt this from a young age. We lived in a loving home in which my parents helped neighbours, families, and sick relatives. Mum and Dad took care of two children for a family whose son was killed instantly in a car accident. They looked after the father and children of a local family when their mum walked out on them. Mum and Dad carried on helping others while dealing with their own grief about the death of their parents. Dad helped drunkards clean up their lives and let them live in the farmhouse*

Discerning shame and speaking the truth 65

and paid them to work for him – many things I learned from watching my parents. But I also believe that child sexual abuse, and from that, the verbal abuse, taught me to look past the skin and see and know when people are hurting, lost, lonely, outcasts. I know what that feels like! I have also worked in pastoral care and advocacy over the past twenty-two years; I believe I looked after, cared deeply for and prayed for every client.

TIM: *How important are these abilities to you? Do you value them in others?*

DALE: *They are extremely important to me, and yes it is rare, but I do really appreciate these abilities in others.*

TIM: *What abilities have assisted you to overcome the effects of shame? For example, expression through art …*

DALE: *Thank you for bringing these questions before me Tim. Caroline [Dale's wife] and I are miniaturists and we have just started a small business in selling dollhouse hardware. We have been preparing for a miniature and dollhouse show. I have been making miniature blankets and rustic wheelbarrows filled with miniature succulents made from cardboard, plus packaging up the hardware and stapling our product topper, logo and price on each packet. I have used this time to mentally escape into each project … so I'm thinking maybe I should use this as an escape when I can …*

Enabling Dale to talk about his skills and abilities in this way made visible a further recognition of his values and what he stood for: 'A recognition that shame is controlling – a liar. It has been and still is … and in a split second, it's able to control me – my thoughts, words – where I instantly go to a place of being flooded with shame'. However, Dale could now visualise the richness of the trunk where looking at the trunk without shame brought about thoughts of acceptance, letting go, awareness of sensations, listening, faith in Jesus, freedom.

We then went on to explore the branches, which represented the hopes, dreams and wishes that Dale has for the direction of his life.

TIM: *What steps will you take regarding uncovering the truth behind shame? What are your intentions behind this?*

DALE: *To share the truth whenever and wherever I feel led. Not allowing shame to control me makes the truth less painful. When you talk about things like this … there are risks … like rejection … being judged … people avoiding you … and not trusting you anymore…. and I find that those feelings are stronger amongst Christians or my church community. So do I take that on or do I leave? Or do I just try and accept that distrust and let them work on that themselves? So there is careful consideration in who I share this with. There is an essence of needing to be heard as well, and I think that comes from being alone and silenced in this for forty years.*

We then focused on the leaves of the tree. The intention of this part of the Tree of Life was to get Dale thinking about the contributions others have made to his life, and how he has impacted others in a positive way.

TIM: *How have they contributed to your understanding of what's right and wrong?*

DALE: *Tim, Robert, my friend Jane and my family have had faith in me and have listened, walked alongside me and believed the truth. Ridsdale had instilled in me that no one*

66 *Discerning shame and speaking the truth*

> *would believe the truth ... and that was not true. So, sharing the truth, speaking it out, to people who hear it ... helps unravels the web of what is right and wrong.*

TIM: *How have you contributed to their lives? What would they want to say, if they were in the room today?*

DALE: *I would be happy to listen to what you would have to say about me Tim ... but I believe Robert would say the things he said in the excerpt from his message. I know what my family and Jane think of me, they love me unconditionally and know I was badly affected by violent childhood sexual abuse, but by finally speaking about this, they have witnessed the effects on me, and I have witnessed the effects on them through the little they know ... so I did not want to have my past affect them any more deeply than it already has. I hope I have contributed to their lives ... by sharing the truth, and I know that my story has impacted their lives; some of that impact has been a good thing and some effects have been negative. Family would say they support me and love me unconditionally, but they want me to move on and forget that this happened.*

At the end of our conversation, we identified the people in Dale's life who reminded him how important it was for him to share the truth of his experience of sexual violence – and for his 'renewed sense of who I am' which was now becoming his dominant story – that is, a person who knows the difference between right and wrong and how sharing the truth can release the effects of shame (Table 9.1).

Further to these conversations Dale shared that 'we can often become muffled between the downs and forget there's been some nice people who accept you'. The follow-up session explored the people Dale named on the leaves of his Tree of Life, who acknowledged and appreciated him sharing the truth. Taking away from these conversations, Dale shared:

- *The leaves puts people in places I didn't know they'd be*
- *Acknowledges these people contributing to me knowing what's right and wrong*
- *Helps along the journey*

The fruits of Dale's tree were then explored, identifying legacies and learnings from now being able to talk about his integrity in such an honouring way.

TIM: *What have you learnt about your integrity?*
DALE: *I have learnt that my integrity has always been there fighting for what's right ...*
TIM: *What type of fruit would be on the tree?*
DALE: *Lemons.*
TIM: *Can I ask why lemons ... bittersweet to the sharing of the truth?*
DALE: *Exactly ... feeling less shame, by being able to share the truth, from my experiences of sexual violence.*

Following the session where Dale had identified his fruits as lemons, I emailed him further questions regarding the tree's flowers, inviting him to consider the legacies that he would like to pass on to others who have also experienced sexual violence.

Discerning shame and speaking the truth 67

Table 9.1 People of significance who have reminded Dale of the significance of him sharing the truth

My brother	Thinking about his relationship differently	Dale's ability to get his brother to look deeper into what an intimate relationship means for him
Friend	Being open and accepting	Acknowledging and appreciating Dale's openness and acceptance of him
Friend	Having a sense of what it is to be free	Dale allowing his friend to feel free in her thoughts and actions
Friend	Appreciating the truth	Appreciation of Dale's honesty of sharing the effects of his experience of being wronged. Dale standing up for what's right
Neighbour	Courage	Acknowledging Dale's courage in standing up for what's right
Practitioner	Being struck by Dale's authentic nature and faith	Dale reminds the practitioner of the need to place faith at the centre of all decisions
Minister	Thanks for sharing the truth	Thankful of Dale's openness

TIM: *How would you like to contribute to others, in a meaningful way, knowing what you now know about your own experiences of shame?*

DALE: *I would like to contribute by getting to know other men who have experienced child sexual violence and be a part of that trusted space where hearts and truths meet, common ground … where we are supported and not judged, accepted, understood … a space where shame can be overcome and the truths of sexual violence can be spoken about freely.*

TIM: *What contributions are you currently making to others in uncovering the truth of shame?*

DALE: *I think that I have definitely helped enable my friend Robert to feel the freedom of being able to speak about the secret truths of the past, by sharing how I am feeling and sharing glimpses of my experiences of the past. I believe as soon as I allowed myself to speak to Robert about these things, it opened the way for us to share, and we knew we were both completely understood, which enabled even more for us to speak openly with freedom. I am one of the people who prays for anyone who needs it after church … I have found in the last while … that as people share their need, I have been able to pray with them in an amazing way because I believe God has given me such understanding. When I am given the opportunity, I am beginning to speak about the truths of shame that are hidden in other people's perception or naive views on certain issues – not necessarily child sexual abuse or my experiences of child sexual abuse but many things that*

68 *Discerning shame and speaking the truth*

sit around that … like Christian views or protocols, the meaning of truth and what it looks like. And shame comes into many things, like being told you haven't been a good father, husband, wife, etc. Shame is involved in many ways and in so many hurts, and I can see shame always seems to hide the truth and the person suffering with shame can't find the truth in their situation … not until they realise what shame is doing …

It was now possible to explore the textual heritage of these survivor skills Dale had identified earlier in our conversations. Again, I invited Dale to tell a story about one of the survival skills or strengths in the roots of his tree. My intention was for Dale to add further context and meaning to his reclaimed experience of living with integrity.

TIM: *Is there an image that represents a skill and its heritage that you have placed on the roots of your tree?*

DALE: *Fight for Justice – Purpose – Fairness.*

I begin with this image of a happy, carefree young boy holding Jesus' hand – some-times I'm walking, running, swinging my arms, singing, sometimes skipping – when all of a sudden my feet fall off – [this was the] first time I was sexually abused. This is painful, shameful – I don't look or feel the same anymore. Jesus walks with me, but every time I step from that moment, more of my body falls off. I can't walk anymore so I drag myself, using my arms, only for a short while, because as I move I lose my hands, arms … this continues until all that is left is my voice, and for myself … I have been silenced. Jesus is with me!!! I hope I am invisible but that's not the case; it doesn't stop people from judgement, names, lies, pain.

Looking around the school yard I became aware there were other kids who were hurt-ing, who were unpopular and had difficult lives, so I worked hard trying to reach out to these kids and make friends with them. I believe that because of the sexual abuse and being silenced, Jesus gave me the gift and the voice to reach out in a way that looked deeper than skin, past the tears to see where they came from, and I wanted in some small way to achieve giving back, taking away injustice which then gave them purpose, and I at least showed that the world was not all about judgement and that there was acceptance giving them back fairness and a better happier life – even if only for moments in time. I reached out with what I thought was nothingness and amazing strength was given back to them and they knew that at least I loved them …

The final part of the Tree of Life activity involved adding to the compost heap. During this process, it is worth considering the type of compost heap used and its significance – for instance, open air, enclosed etc. The compost heap gave Dale the opportunity to write down anything that would normally go in the other sections of the tree, but which were now things he no longer wanted to be defined by. Dale had the opportunity to write down places, people, problems, experiences, which can often be sources of trauma, abuse, cultural standards of normality / beauty / etc. or anything else that shapes negative thoughts about himself in his mind. Dale added the following experiences:

DALE: *What I have added to the compost heap could have been more. This is what I have decided to share:*

Discerning shame and speaking the truth   69

- *Some people in the church including Ridsdale, the Catholic hierarchy, legal team and psychiatrist*
- *Grief – loss of childhood*
- *Low self-worth and trust in man*
- *Footy training – kicks up the arse.*

Further to Dale's sharing, a question was posed to him about the contents of the compost heap.

TIM: *When we refer to what you have added to the compost heap, do they stay and go back into the soil because they further add to your integrity, for example?*

DALE: *I must say I struggled with this concept – and I could have put so many more things into the compost – because I thought as I took part in this action of placing people, problems, experiences, or anything else that shapes negative thoughts into the compost heap, that I was literally dealing with these traumas. But after a short while, I was shocked to realise that these things cannot be just thrown into the compost and be forgotten about because they are all part of who I am. When you experience something like childhood sexual violence, it – and all it entails – becomes part of who you are. So they definitely go back into the soil, and help to feed the truth; my narrative can never change. My ultimate hope is that I will learn to live with the truth and also with the freedom to talk about my truth in the hope it will help someone else to know that freedom. To me, that says there is such a richness in the soil from the compost heap. The Tree of Life is such a worthwhile and fascinating project to go through, and to realise that the growth processes of a tree to the compost heap have brought an undeniable richness to my story.*

During this process of releasing the effects of shame using the Tree of Life activity, what was made possible for Dale was that he now had a voice and could speak up against the effects of sexual violence with a stronger foundation built upon his own lived experiences.

TIM: *What has been made possible from this sharing of the truth, in this way?*

DALE: *It has allowed me to speak about my experiences of violent childhood sexual abuse. Now I have a deep understanding of the way shame works, I can overcome shame's power, so it is not in control – and that plays a big part in not being silenced.*

Often we are responding to the effects of not only individual trauma, but of collective trauma. According to Denborough (2008, p. 23): 'The nature of conventional therapeutic practices promoting conversations that are kept within the four walls of therapy, have the potential to overwhelmingly listen for, attend to, and build upon individualist speech patterns, which can make assumptions'. This is not suggesting that conventional therapeutic practices do not have a place, as my practice is predominantly in this setting. My hope is that the material Dale and I present in this book, *Reclaiming lives from sexual violence*, affirms the benefit of sharing one's experience with others. Further, by noticing and responding to openings and invitations a person can make in terms of linking their experiences to broader

70 *Discerning shame and speaking the truth*

Figure 9.1 Whiteboard notes of Dale describing lived experiences where he is not alone.

collectives, enabling them to make contributions regarding social issues that have affected their own life and the lives of others, is equally of benefit (Figure 9.1).

Following the Tree of Life activity, Dale and I decided to deconstruct what sharing the truth meant for him. The conversation was externalised by using the whiteboard, and we were both able to co-contribute to the conversation and build upon Dale's lived experiences and explore what it would mean to contribute to others through a collective action. With Dale's understanding that he is not alone, Dale shared that there is:

> ... *a freedom to speak about your experience with other people who understand. That is a vital thing for someone who has been silenced for years and years. To be finally speaking about the sexual violence, and shame not controlling you – that's an amazing freedom.*

Many of the people we consult with have little opportunity to feel as if they are making a contribution to the lives of others. The person may feel despair and anguish in the struggle to get their own life together, let alone being able to offer something to someone else. However, the difficulties that people are facing will not be theirs alone, and their experiences of oppression and how they have responded to the hurt can offer a contribution to others in similar or related situations. Significantly, the experience of inputting into the lives of others can be the catalyst to reduce the effects (or transform the nature) of the suffering in the person's life. This realisation can bring a 'sense that their suffering has not been for nothing, which has the potential to ignite a sense of possibility that can swell over to other aspects of their life' Denborough 2008, p. 3).

10 Dale's re-claiming of integrity

"sharing a glimpse of my story with explicit detail"

Key points to consider

- <u>Providing space for the client to share their lived experiences</u>: *The significance of the practitioner being vulnerable and compassionate when walking alongside the client.*
- <u>The client reclaiming their integrity:</u> *The client unlocking shame and sharing their truths from their experiences of sexual violence.*
- <u>Placing value on listening to the client's explicit accounts of childhood sexual violence:</u> *Being committed and open to believing the client's story and seeing the reality of why survivors of childhood sexual violence are experts in their own lived experiences.*

My story has been locked in silence for forty-two years, until now. Prior to my walk with Tim, I had lived a life of silent brokenness – shattered and confused in so many ways, controlled by shame, guilt and the endless traumatic fallout after being violently sexually abused as a child. I was eleven years old when the abuse began, and the abuse continued over a period of twenty-eight months. The perpetrator was Father Gerald Ridsdale, the local Catholic priest in Inglewood, Victoria, at that time.

This book, *Reclaiming lives from sexual violence*, is more than a record of the therapeutic journey in narrative therapy Tim and I embarked on – for me, it goes deeper than that. This is my story of unlocking shame, reclaiming integrity and finally sharing my truth. It is also a glimpse of the explicit detail, that heinous detail that sits behind the words – 'sexual violence'. Sharing this detail is profoundly significant for me – as it is, I believe, profoundly significant for anyone who has been violently sexually abused as a child. I wouldn't have the ability to speak about my story right now if it wasn't for Tim and the way he has worked with such vulnerability in and through our narrative therapy journey, in such an amazingly sensitive, caring way. Over time, I gained a deeper understanding of shame, enabling me to reclaim my integrity and break shame's power – also breaking the silence I had held for forty-two years, allowing me to speak openly.

To give you some context to the importance of this book, it is crucial for me to start when the abuse began. I began to appreciate that sharing the explicit detail is extremely important for anyone who has been sexually abused as a child, to release the effects of the abuse. It's important because the power of shame and guilt lies in the explicit – and in the words spoken over you by the perpetrator. As I was given

DOI: 10.4324/9781003256816-11

72 *Dale's re-claiming of integrity*

the ability to release the explicit detail, I was able to walk through the experiences again, to stand on them, examine and observe them. Facing the experiences releases the truth, which allowed me to see my innocence and to understand that the sexual violence, is not – and was never – my fault.

I hope my story can give the reader insight into the way Tim has worked in and through narrative therapy with sensitivity and vulnerability. I hope sharing this explicit detail will help whoever reads this book gain an understanding of the world of a person who has been violently sexually abused. I also want to speak up for the silent survivors, in the hope it will encourage them to come forward, break their long-held silence and reclaim their integrity. I know when I broke my silence and spilled my experiences out in the right space, I felt such freedom – from the shame-filled explicit detail which was no longer held in the dark silence inside of me, but which was now outside of me; it was now 'out there'. Shame had been broken. Sharing detail at the right time, with the right person, in the right space, brings so much freedom. I hope my story can help professionals and survivors into the future.

Sharing the explicit detail may be challenging to hear; it may not be considered central to the conversation; but for me and other sexual abuse survivors, I believe it is paramount – when facilitated in a careful, sensitive and attentive manner – because it is the truth.

When I listen to programs about sexual violence, it feels like the words themselves – 'sexual violence' – are being thrown around like a balloon at a party, and the meaning to the term then loses significance – like any other overused words – potentially causing a skimming-over of the horrendous detail that lies behind them. Thus, I want to give you a glimpse of the explicit meaning I place in the words 'sexual violence'. What you will read next details my first experiences while in the (perceived) trustworthy hands of Gerald Ridsdale. This is what happened; these are my truths. I was a child, he was an adult in a position of authority. The reality of sexual abuse needs to be made public – even though challenging to hear, it is also extremely challenging to share.

Thus, I hope my revealing in this way will prepare you when you are working with other survivors of sexual abuse. The fact is, statistically, there is a strong possibility you may come across a person who has experienced sexual abuse in your work; this is the reality. Maybe my experiences are even closer for you. Maybe you are a survivor of childhood sexual violence yourself, or the parent, friend, or sibling of a survivor. I've been closed for a long time – I'm now allowing myself to be honest. I will keep sharing …

A glimpse of my story with explicit detail

The abuse began six weeks before my twelfth birthday. I remember that day like it was yesterday – in the office of the Inglewood Catholic presbytery, Ridsdale violently sexually abused me. I was invited by some boys I went to school with to the after-school program Ridsdale had started; there were about twenty-five boys in the billiard room that day. Ridsdale was sitting in a chair placed near the doorway that led to the bathroom. I needed to go to the toilet, and as I went to pass Ridsdale's chair, he grabbed me and pulled me in to sit between his legs. He quickly put his arms over my shoulders, crossing his hands and putting them over my groin. Ridsdale was strong – he pulled me in tight and proceeded to fondle my genitals. I didn't know what in the hell was going on. Ridsdale was whispering and kissing my ear which tickled, then after a few minutes, he pushed me out of the chair with his crutch. Holding my hand tightly, he took me into his office, which was on the right-hand side at the front of the house. There was a lit display cabinet full of beautiful, polished stones and opals. He walked me around them, then he took me to his desk, knelt down in front of me and kissed me passionately over my mouth. It was yuk – I hated it. Then he pulled my pants and underwear down, lifted me up onto his desk and started to lick and suck my testicles and my penis, while fingering my anus. Something happened to my penis inside his mouth – it was a sensation I had not experienced before – I was petrified … I thought he was going to eat me, and that something was dreadfully wrong with me. I was shaking and filled with fear, and the confusion and mental torment this created was devastating – my life changed in an instant. I lost my identity, my innocence, my childhood, my voice – I was confused, frightened, covered in shame and guilt. Ridsdale cleaned me up and then, while pulling up my underwear and pants, he said, 'I love you Dale, this is our secret. I don't want you to talk about this to anyone, not a word. I am trusted in this community, and your parents trust me too – if you talk about this, you will be punished by God. Not a word to anyone, OK'. Then he took me back into the billiard room, pushing me through the door … leaving me there, while closing the door behind me. I stood there bewildered, shaking uncontrollably, with every eye in the room upon me. The boys were sniggering and pointing – they obviously knew something had happened to me. I made my way slowly out of the house and ran home as fast as my body would allow. I went to my room and sobbed uncontrollably, feeling the warmth of Jesus' presence holding me close. From that day on, school was a nightmare. I was bullied – physically and verbally abused on a daily basis. They called me a poofter and Ridsdale's bum-boy and other associated names. On top of Ridsdale's cautioning words, I believed I must be what they were calling me – and that I was to blame – which covered me in shame and silenced me. That was the first of many times I was violently sexually abused by Gerald Ridsdale. I went on many trips with him – panning for gold; searching for precious stones; fossicking for opals in White Cliffs, NSW; a visit to Clunes staying at the Clunes Catholic Presbytery overnight; and a trip to Ballarat to see Ridsdale's parents and visit a well-known Catholic priest. These trips are all significant in my story.

★★

Significantly, my faith has never wavered. Many times while being violently sexually abuse by Ridsdale, I thought I would die or I was dead. I believe I am alive today because Jesus saved me, and for this reason, I want to give praise and glory to Jesus my Saviour and Lord, praising Him also for giving Tim and me the obedience, ability and direction to document our journey. This is our story, with Tim 'walking' beside me through the process of narrative therapy.

74   *Dale's re-claiming of integrity*

It's extraordinary, the way in which this collaboration came into being. I had just experienced my second court appearance, in a case against Catholic priest Gerald Ridsdale for childhood sexual abuse. I was struggling deeply. After the court appearance, I met a social worker from the Office of Public Prosecutions who made an appointment for me at a sexual assault agency. Incredibly, it happened to be the agency where Tim had just taken up a position. This is when our journey began.

Tim, I am indebted to you for your professionalism and incredible knowledge – the way you work with such innovation, understanding, care, compassion, vulnerability and sensitivity. It was December 2014 when I first started seeing you, and it is now 2021, so thank you for your dedication and the time you have put into 'walking alongside' me. You created a space for me where I was believed, with no judgement or detrimental comments or assumptions ever made. With other counsellors and psychologists prior to and during the court process, I endured horrendous treatment, soul-destroying judgements and comments, and an environment where I wasn't believed.

Tim – you led me in the direction of my truth, which was hidden deeply and controlled by shame and guilt, keeping me in a place of dark defeat, self-hate, blame and silence for forty-two years. You worked gently, asking the right questions, and we shared the whiteboard note-taking that formed the basis for this book.

When you interviewed me as 'Shame', it was painful, yet extraordinary, and it awakened my integrity, pulling me out of a deep dark pit covered in shit, bringing me into the light, wanting to live again. Because of the way you worked with me through the process of Narrative Therapy, with absolute consideration and care for the client, I now have a deep understanding of the way shame works and can fight through its power to break the silence and talk about my story of childhood sexual violence. Breaking my silence with this deeper understanding of shame has brought such freedom to me. Thank you.

★★

Tim and I hope that all survivors of childhood sexual violence or other traumatic experiences can come to know this same freedom. We have worked together sharing our stories at several conferences around Australia, and have now co-authored this book, *Reclaiming lives from sexual violence*. This brings to life our hope that, by sharing Tim's innovative work in the field of narrative therapy, and my story as the client, to the mental health industry and to those working and/or studying in this field, we can offer this potential path to freedom to others who are suffering.

11 The joining of stories as a political act

Key points to consider

- <u>Thinking about a client's experiences as something political</u>: *Providing a space for people to find their 'voice' and 'authentic self'.*

Nearing the end of Dale and I 'walking alongside' each other, I was inspired by the writings of Renee Handsacker (2012). Renee encouraged me to think about Dale's experience as something political, which needed to be shared with other men who had had similar experiences. If one of the purposes of counselling is to provide a space for people to find their 'voice' and their 'authentic self', my role would not be to contain these conversations, so as to ensure they remained 'safe', but rather to expand them and enable the sharing of stories with others. My hope with Dale was to provide a space for him to meet with another male, with the intention of further releasing the effects of shame in both their lives and to contribute to their preferred ways of being. Also, for this exchange to challenge the dominant beliefs and assumptions in society that place expectations on what it means to be a male in today's world – that is, as far as Dale and other men who have experienced significant acts of oppression *can* share about their experiences, when given the opportunity to do so.

Without a collaborative effort in uncovering Dale's truths of his experiences of sexual violence, reclaiming his life with a deeper understanding of shame would not have been made possible. Drawing attention to and shedding light on those dominant discourses that influenced shame made it possible to reduce shame's power in keeping Dale silent. Furthermore, ideas of self and life are continuously negotiated through the communities, experiences and paradigms we live amongst (White 2003). Hilde Lindemann Nelson (2001, p. 13) describes identities as 'collaborative ventures requiring a number of people to bring them into being'. Our identity is social and relational and we make meaning of ourselves and our lives through others (Handsacker 2012). By inviting two adult men to collaborate and to speak of their own resonance, knowledge and understandings, we hoped to expose new territories regarding what is possible to know and act upon (White 2005) (Table 11.1).

DOI: 10.4324/9781003256816-12

76   *The joining of stories as a political act*

Table 11.1 The significance of creating space for two males to share the truth

Tim	Dale	John
What does it mean to be able to speak about the truths of your experiences of sexual violence?	It means that after forty-two years of silenced inner turmoil on many shame-covered truths of violent sexually abusive experiences, I am now able to speak … verbalising these truths by breaking through shame; because in verbalising these things, the truth is realised in a new way … uncovering the lies that the abuser spoke over me … realising the truth that … the sexual violence was not my fault; it was not my punishment; I was not naughty, or sinful or a liar … and that family or other people would not believe me if I told them about the sexual violence … such lies that I believed. Child sexual violence is not easy to talk about but all this means that child sexual violence needs to be talked about … enabling those surviving sexual violence to release the information from the locked dungeon inside and putting it out there …	The ability to speak about my abuse means a number of things actually. Recognising the abuse myself, I am able to now manage the negative thoughts better around self-loathing and self-disrespect. I am also able to recognise that the abuse was not my fault, that it was something that was forced upon me and out of my control. And in speaking about it has brought with it increased confidence within myself and a strength to speak up when I feel something is perhaps wrong or incorrect.
What would it mean for others, who have also experienced similar acts of violence, to be able to hear your story?	I have really only heard … other men's and women's stories in court cases. I found this process to be horrific, painfully emotional … because in the court process it is very clinical and there is no one to support … it absolutely takes such strength and control not to vomit with the pain of knowing what each victim	The only way I can answer this is to explain what it would mean to me to be able to hear others' stories. I don't mean to pigeon-hole people, and one should never place one's own feelings upon someone else; however, I believe there would be a feeling of relief. Not a relief that someone else went through something like me,

Continued

The joining of stories as a political act 77

Table 11.1 (Continued)

Tim	Dale	John
	was going through. I just wanted to get up and hold those people while they spoke, and I knew I had to get up and share when my name was called … I felt numb … I have also shared some glimpses of my story to a friend who has experienced sexual violence from Ridsdale and he has shared some glimpses of his story to me. This has happened over quite a few conversations, but I believe in those glimpses of sharing we have both felt supported, understood, accepted; we both felt some healing, and freedom … which was an amazing feeling. We questioned why we had never shared anything before … but came to the conclusion that it would never have been right until now and put it down to God's timing …	as no one should have gone through it in the first place, but a relief that I am not the only one or that I am alone in this journey. I have never really been alone as I reckon I have wonderful support around me but I don't or haven't had the opportunity – this may be a bad word in this context but can't think of another – to discuss my abuse with other survivors. As I indicated above though, this is really what I would feel to hear someone else's story so it may be wildly different to what others might feel.
How does sharing your story contribute to challenging the dominant beliefs and assumptions of what it means to be a man (and loving father in today's world?)	… what does it mean to be a man??? A man took away my sexual innocence, my childhood and stole my sexual being… . I am a man but does that mean anything … ? I have been accused of being many things, but one thing I am sure of is … I would never want to be a man that sexually abused anyone … child or adult … I see myself as not having a gender … but I am confused about that because many elements of sexual violence hold me in a place of not ever needing or wanting to	I guess this has been an issue most of my adult life. As a result of my abuse, I believe I have questioned my place in the world of men. I have struggled to mix with men and even really place myself on the same level as other men. I don't know if this is a trust thing or something else, but there has never been a real comfort for me in the company of other men. This was one of the most challenging issues I had to face when my first two children were boys; how would I manage to be a father to them when they became men? There is a

Continued

78 *The joining of stories as a political act*

Table 11.1 (Continued)

Tim	Dale	John
	experience sex. Does that make me less of a man? Does that mean I am not good at being a man … husband??? Nevertheless, I believe I am a good, loving but overprotective father – and a father who would go to the ends of the earth to protect my children. I can reflect on what an amazing father my father was, but he failed in protecting me, and I have failed in protecting one of my children … I say my dad was an amazingly wonderful father and my children have all thanked me for being a wonderful dad, and they would never say I failed them … so am I a loving father? Yes, I think I am, and I am committed to that and continue to do my best.	strange thing with kids though, and it's about unconditional love they have for their parents, and I don't think they could love me any more or any less than they do. I grew up when life was a lot about turning the other cheek and putting up with things and I think this added to my inability to disclose for so long, as there was always that voice saying to be a man and put up with it. It is only in more recent times that I have realised (and this may be more age related than anything else) that you don't have to put up with it; if it is wrong, it is wrong – plain and simple.
What has been made possible by you sharing your story with someone who has also experienced sexual violence?	It made possible – out of mutual heartfelt concern, love, care and understanding – a non–judgemental space opening … a way for me to share some extremely intimate details of sexual violence … like stepping out onto common ground. My sharing made it possible for the other person to share, and I have shared Robert's response in previous notes where he expresses beautifully what my sharing meant to him. I think I would explain it like being blind for forty years and instantly regaining sight … or mute for forty years and regaining the ability to speak. Can you imagine what that's like?	I will have to reserve my thoughts on this one, but my gut tells me that I would feel what I have discussed in the second point above.

The joining of stories as a political act   79

After careful consideration of how to commence these conversations, the following questions were asked of Dale and John, who was also a client of the sexual assault agency. They exchanged their responses through emails (facilitated through me), enabling the sharing of stories of resistance and hope. A further meeting between these two men in the context of sharing their experiences didn't eventuate, yet being given the space to share their truths with someone else proved to be quite significant. I have included both their responses below. What did eventuate though was an adult men's group where the Tree of Life activity was undertaken, and which both Dale and John attended. Prior to them sharing the truth, I asked them both what it meant to them to be sharing their truths with another male regarding the sexual violence. And was it okay to do so? Dale was able to share:

> I just wanted to answer your question regarding sharing the truth with another adult male ... and I believe my answer is yes, I am happy to do that, and I would be happy to continue conversing with them into the future. I have one concern and that is my apprehension about trusting other males ... which I do try hard to work on and have a growing yearning to be able to trust men again. I just guess I would hate them to feel that from me, which is my greatest concern ... but in thinking about it they will have their internal issues as well. In a positive sense I look forward to sharing my story and hearing another share their story, and I do believe sharing the truth with another who understands is an important access to releasing the shame that builds up, and it's even more important to begin that process to freedom by sharing with someone who understands and has experienced sexual violence.

Even though a follow-up meeting did not eventuate between Dale and John, the fostering of this opportunity promoted the idea that by actively taking these issues out of the private sphere, a sense of collective action can be made possible. This creates movement towards a response in counselling that encourages people to be able to support each other and communities. Reaching new identity conclusions through joining lives, people's identities are shaped by the contexts into which they are born and continue to be surrounded by and interact with (Handsacker 2012). Picking the right time in the session to promote a broader thinking of the individual's experiences is crucial and not paying attention to our influence could potentially create a shifting of power back with the practitioner, by unintentionally centring ourselves back in the conversation. There are days when the thoughts of the person seeing me need prioritising, days when I have needed to hold the individual conversation with the person's experiences of sexual violence or oppressive acts they had experienced – for instance, the ups and downs associated with being reminded of their experiences of sexual violence, and the need to talk about safety. At times I have found myself getting too far ahead in our conversations, and I have needed to de-centre myself and become curious again.

80 *The joining of stories as a political act*

★★

> What actions do you currently take to catch yourself out when your own agenda becomes centred in the conversation?

★★

12 Making visible the signs of social and psychological resistance

Key points to consider

- <u>Highlighting social and psychological resistance</u>: *Increasing the client's personal agency.*

The hope was that, through sharing with another adult male, Dale would be placed in a position of power, which would give him personal agency and a unified place to stand where he would no longer be silenced. Challenging dominant ways of working therapeutically continued to unfold in my practice. Dale and John's sharing of stories about resistance to the sexual violence was limited due to the constraints of email and not having met each other face to face. Therefore, as a response to Dale's experiences, and trying to make further sense of the power and influence of the effects of shame on his life, I adapted a checklist used by David Denborough (2008) within the context of war and armed conflict. This checklist was used to highlight social and psychological resistance, which is a process of ongoing development for Dale. The checklist built on our previous conversations, and continued to increase Dale's personal agency, which was not based on a one-size-fits-all assessment, as is often used in the clinical services area.

With questions about how, when and where he showed signs of resistance, the checklist gave Dale the opportunity for further meaning making, enabling him to add detail to his history of resistance.

★★

> You may have further questions to add to this tool, I would encourage you to do this.

★★

DOI: 10.4324/9781003256816-13

82   *Making visible the signs*

These visible signs of physical and psychological resistance have been shared with others with great positive outcomes: 'This sort of sharing can sustain social and psychological resistance in even the hardest of circumstances' (Denborough 2008, p. 135). Refer to Appendix H for a template of this tool, to use in your own practice (Table 12.1).

Table 12.1 Signs of social and psychological resistance

PART 1: DURING THE EXPERIENCES OF SEXUAL VIOLENCE

Tried to protect yourself during the experiences of sexual violence: physically and/or emotionally.
  What steps did you take? Some of them you may have already spoken about.
  In the Presbytery, Ridsdale used to play this game of hide and seek, and when he found me, he would force me to perform a sexual act on him. Ridsdale played Benny Hill music during this game. One day he could not find me, he was so angry … and I was so so frightened, but I waited until I knew he was up in the front of the house and I ran out of the back door and into the bush at the side of the hospital … I was so frightened. I stayed in the bush for a while and then walked home, frightened he would find me. When I got home, he was sitting at our kitchen table having a cuppa with Mum and Dad.
  Once I fought to get out of his hold. Ridsdale, in a room with about twenty boys playing pool, I walked past Ridsdale's chair and he pulled me onto his lap, put his arms over my shoulders, and his hands over my genitals and pulled me in tight as he fondled my genitals (he had done this many times before) looking for a sexual response. This time I put up a fight, wriggling and continually putting up a resistance. Ridsdale was whispering and putting his tongue in my ear saying, 'I'm not letting you go, I love you.' I could feel his penis as a hardening lump in my lower back. I was frightened and trying to stop any sexual response on my part. I thrashed around and finally weakened his hold on me. Ridsdale was furious … I broke loose and I ran and ran all the way home.
  This happened towards the end of Ridsdale's time in Inglewood. It was the last time Ridsdale ever touched me. In my police statement, this was the only time I told police about. I was not ready to share or go any deeper into my story … I was so filled with shame about the times I tried to put up a fight, but Ridsdale's anger controlled me with fear.

Displayed acts of caring, concern, comfort for others during the experiences of sexual violence: (may include caring for friends, children or other adults) that allowed you to stand up for what is right in your life.
  Tell me more about these experiences of knowing what was right?
  I don't believe this happened while I was experiencing sexual violence … I didn't comfort others at that time because I was struggling so much to survive myself. I was so confused, and I believe, I knew sexual violence was wrong before I realised what was right …

Received comfort from others during the experiences of sexual violence (was able to take this in):
  I don't believe this happened for me at this time, because no one knew about it, and those that did certainly did not comfort me – they made my situation very much worse.
  Being able to still receive comfort from others – what does this say about you knowing the difference between right and wrong?
  I believe being silent was the only way … that seemed right to me because I was told over and over again by Ridsdale that my parents trusted him and they wouldn't believe me. I knew that was wrong, really, but I was a child. And I believed Ridsdale … fear and shame played a major role in remaining silent.

(Continued)

Making visible the signs 83

Table 12.1 (Continued)

Displayed acts of caring for oneself during the experiences of sexual violence.

Jesus was the only one that comforted or cared for me during this time. The only other thing that I did to try and help myself was to … put on an invisible façade. This mentally prepared me to face another day, enabling me to leave the safety of my family home … believing that I wasn't the person people could see on the outside. The façade hid the inside – the disgusting, violated, dirty, shameful Dale.

How much courage does it take to think about these times?

I can't explain how painful it is to think about my tormented sexually violated childhood/life. It has taken such strength to be here today talking about this … but mentally, after forty years, I find this extremely freeing to talk about …

What things did you do to care for yourself during these times?

Often when I got back to the safety of my family home, I would go to my room or up the bush to our cubby, put myself in Jesus' arms and sob my day away … Jesus understood … and today I just cry – tears are freeing. Sharing written or spoken truths with Tim as he walks beside me in this is freeing and releases me from that which mentally/internally builds up …

Displayed acts of dignity or pride during your experiences of sexual violence: not allowing for the effects of shame to have an influence.

Don't think there were any … because the shameful sexual acts permeated who I was on the inside.

Found ways to hold onto hope during the experiences of sexual violence: may include spiritual, faith practices: having power over the effects of shame

Jesus was my hope, He is why I live today – I lost faith/hope in humanity!

PART 2: AFTER THE EXPERIENCES OF SEXUAL VIOLENCE

Displaying acts of caring, concern, comfort for others after the experiences of sexual violence (may include friends, children or other adults).

Firstly, I never spoke to anyone about my experiences of sexual violence. I was a broken, very sad boy, who was a still silent voice. After my experiences of sexual violence had finished, I had lost my childhood – it was over. I looked at the world around me with a compassion I had not understood before; I looked with a maturity, with my heart, past the skin – and I saw the pain and sadness in other kids who lived difficult lives. They were difficult to be friends with because their home lives didn't allow them to have close friends but I did my best to help and listen …

I made one really good friend with an older girl who was chubby and had a mop of orange fuzzy hair. This friend Rosemary had an older mum. Rosemary's dad had died when she was a little girl, and her mum was eccentric, old fashioned and lived frugally in a big old mansion in which they only lived in the bottom floor. Rosemary's mum allowed me into their lives, they didn't judge me they loved me for who I was … Rosemary and her mum allowed me to cook creatively, paint and wallpaper the upstairs rooms, also to cut their hair. She taught me how to do crossword puzzles and many other things. This was all a form of escapism for me … but I was able to care deeply for them and I believe I made their life much happier …

Receiving comfort from others (is able to take this in): maximising the impacts of value for yourself and others. What do these acts say about what you value?

What are your intentions for receiving comfort from others?

I didn't ever go looking for comfort … but maybe acceptance. It probably gave me comfort knowing I had made Rosemary and her mum's life happier because they knew I loved and cared for them when not many others did …

(Continued)

84 *Making visible the signs*

Table 12.1 (Continued)

Taking steps to try to reclaim things of significance: being aware of the effects of your own values and beliefs and sharing the truth.

There is no reclaiming anything … my childhood was gone, my innocence gone. There is something about child sexual violence for me that never let me forget, even though I pushed it all into the depths of my being …

My daily life at school was horrific with verbal abuse. I never felt like a girl, or a poofter, homosexual etc – those names I was called every day – but when I was called Ridsdale's bum-boy … that was true. In the safety of my home I never slept well … when I closed my eyes my dreams were dominated by the sexual violence. One dream I had every night for thirty years – it was a snake trying to enter me through my anus … often I would wake ejaculating. I was beside myself with fear and confusion most of the time. I hated these dreams I had no control over … my wet dreams were controlled by the sexual violence … I never had a sexually normal wet dream … no peace … not awake or asleep.

I have always had this internal struggle knowing I wasn't homosexual. My dreams were making me believe I was … but I wasn't!!! Kids and adults were accusing me of being gay. I was physically abused, kicked up the bum, pushed over, laughed at. Every time I went to the toilet I bled from the bum …

This has been my secret life I have not spoken about before … so there has been no reclaiming. Yes, I have strong Christian values which have been shattered, but more than that, I have an absolute knowledge that Jesus has walked this road with me and His presence is very real in my life. He has not abandoned me … I have a loving mum and siblings and wife and children and a couple of friends, but they don't know this is my internal secret life's struggle …

Making plans to rebuild parts of your life from what has been silenced / forgotten by your experiences of sexual violence: what are the effects of acknowledging your own values of knowing what's right and wrong making possible in your life?

Now, after forty-odd years of being silenced, I don't feel the need to rebuild my childhood. This is my life … I feel now that I need to break the silence, talk about the truth and to share and hear other people's stories in the hope that they too can break their silence – speaking, spilling our stories outside of us, this has caused me to experience a freedom that I hope for, for others.

From a Christian point of view, Jesus must have a purpose for me … I am blessed, I think, to be still here. Now I must help others and myself by sharing and hopefully learning from others the truth of their deepest secret life … hoping they too can release it. Our future is what needs to be built!!

I personally don't see any benefit of trying to rebuild the past – we are who we are today because of our past – we have to try and build a future, not just for us but for every child in the future to be made aware that sexual abuse is not acceptable … talk about it … so no child will have to live or suffer in silence … ever again!!!

Speaking with others or listening to others about their experiences of sexual violence in ways that contribute to feeling joined and stronger: minimising the effects of shame and strengthening your sharing of the truth.

I really haven't reached that point yet, but I am hoping that an opportunity will open up for me … where I can hopefully spend my life speaking out truthfully about what needs to be known about childhood sexual violence, the effects on the body, the mind and life, and of course listening to others allowing them to speak out from the silence, will … help US to feel that connectedness, joining of experiences, a place of understanding, a place I have not experienced before …

It feels like it will be a place to go, if we can believe, grow in trust of each other and be there for each other when we need to talk. With an understanding of the way shame works, the silence will finish.

Making visible the signs 85

Table 12.1 (Continued)

Able to find joy in small moments within life, minimising the effects of shame, overpowering the effects of shame and allowing for the effects of sharing the truth and knowing right from wrong to be influenced.

I believe this for me is not about rebuilding my life but accepting the life I have had – this has been my life, you cannot change that. Yes, I can and do have moments of joy, and I understand the way shame works. My counsellor Tim has been amazing at helping me deal with shame. I now understand the way shame works … and I have realised that I have carried Ridsdale's shame around for forty years. It is not mine and never has been, but sadly, it has controlled my life for a very long time.

I am not free of shame but I understand the way it works. I also have my own shame which was strongest in my sexual response to being sexually stimulated by Ridsdale or ejaculating … or the dreams [mentioned before] …

My shame made me believe the truth was too shameful – and knowing right from wrong gave shame even greater strength. But now shame has been broken, broken from the guilt of being involved in the sexual violence …. and now my knowledge of the truth is free to be spoken about …

Linking with others through song, music, prayer, art and so on, to share experiences, sorrows, hopes and dreams: allowing for your values and beliefs to be influenced.

I have not experienced this.

Finding ways to take action either individually or with others that are in accord with what hopes or dreams you have for your life: exploring the effects that your knowledge of sharing the truth and knowing what's right is having on future decisions.

I have a great desire to help other men who have experienced sexual violence as a child to enter a space where there is freedom from the silence … freedom to be understood, not judged … freedom to be heard … listened to and believed.

If I can help other men, then I feel that there was a reason for me to have lived this life, a reason why I experienced sexual abuse as a child … and a reason why I have to accept the life I have had and help build a future for many …

Rather than using this form of assessment at the commencement of our initial journey together, I chose to use this way of hearing Dale's stories of resistance towards the end of our walk together. Dale's responses highlight the importance of being vulnerable; as practitioners, sometimes we will not obtain the responses we have intended. Dale's account is raw and honest, and my use of the assessment tool brought about an openness for Dale where he was sharing his truths – not what I wanted to hear. I thank Dale for that.

★★

Dale hopes that you may use this checklist with the people you may be consulting with, and he would love to hear about how it goes.

★★

If you can respond with the truth, it is definitely going to help you – it gives you insight into yourself.

(Dale Johns 2020)

13 Dale moving out into the world with confidence in knowing the truth and having a deeper understanding of shame

Key points to consider:

- <u>Coming to a close</u>: *Increasing possibilities for clients to be the ones who decide when the therapeutic journey should come to a close.*

Over time, for Dale and me, our walk together gained greater clarity and purpose. We were now able to locate Dale's individual experiences of sexual violence as a community issue requiring a community-placed initiative. Dale was now committed to, in his words, 'stop the silence and stop the sexual abuse'. An example of this is Dale's commitment to being interviewed in a private hearing at the Royal Commission into Institutional Responses to Childhood Sexual Abuse. A while before the hearing, Dale had reflected that he was 'just going to be telling the truth', but as the hearing drew closer, Dale was able to give further meaning behind him 'just telling the truth' and what was now being made possible:

> … to tell the truth is important, and even though as painful as it was to hold onto what happened to me, the protection of others outweighed that pain. For example, thinking I can't live with this and changing my appearance, so others couldn't see the effects of the acts on me, or so I felt. It must have been God to help do that. Now not being silenced is an acceptance of who I am and the importance I now place on telling the truth, free from shame, and to challenge society's myths around sexual violence. Because I can't change who I am … and I don't want to. It's not about forming a new identity construction but a renewed sense of who I am. That's the truth … I can just be me, I have to be, I am going to be.

Dale's wanting to contribute to others to 'stop the silence … stop the sexual abuse' had been strengthened. Dale's preferred way of telling the truth was given further meaning as we explored the potential of writing down his story and sharing it with others.

> I am very happy for you to send this information … and if it is going to contribute to my story and help a nation stop the silence behind sexual abuse, I am all for it … that is why I have to believe that God allowed me to go through the

DOI: 10.4324/9781003256816-14

Dale moving out into the world 87

violent sexual abuse. There must be a purpose – and if that's part of the purpose, that brings even more understanding to why He did what he did …

Increasing possibilities for people who consult with us to be the ones who decide when the therapeutic journey should come to a close is worth considering. Finding the best time, ways and words to negotiate this can be hazardous in nature. So, what does 'come to a close' mean, in the context of a therapeutic alliance that may have been formed over a considerable time? There are pressures for the practitioner to become centralised, taking control of the 'discharge' or 'termination' process, and in so doing, removing this power from the family or the person we are consulting (White 2003). When space is made available for family members to engage in the retelling of experiences that are associated with the more preferred stories of their lives, and there is acknowledgement of these preferred claims connected with these performances, the practitioner becomes increasingly decentralised in the whole process, and eventually they are discharged from the therapy (White 1995).

I'd like to share a conversation I had with a young person and his mother. Picking up the subtleties in the conversation can be beneficial, yet there is a need to proceed with caution.

TIM: *So, thank you again for the conversations today. How do you think these conversations are going?*

BRIAN: *Yep* … [with a pondering look towards Mum]

TIM: *What are your thoughts on continuing these sessions fortnightly? Or do you have any other ideas?*

BRIAN: *Mmmm … not really sure* [again … looking towards Mum]

TIM: *You know it's okay if you don't need me in your life anymore?*

BRIAN: [with a smile] … *I didn't want to hurt your feelings or anything … but* [with prompting from Mum] *I reckon I'll be okay. Is that okay?*

TIM: *Of course it is, and thank you again Brian, for allowing me in your life. You know that I am always here. And wow … even during this time, you are thinking of others.*

It is crucial in the therapeutic walk together to recognise the impact of the journey affects both client and practitioner. In my walk with Dale over three and a half years, I needed to recognise that our sharing was a privilege and to understand what it meant for my values and for the reason I chose to be a social worker. I had to recognise that I was also impacted by Dale's story. This required me to be open to acknowledging the shift in my thinking about sexual abuse and what it meant for me as a father and husband. Acknowledging the impact when drawing to the end of a therapeutic relationship is a two-way process, and care needs to be taken for both parties. I was therefore required to be vulnerable in my assessment of self – and that was okay.

Continual evaluation of our practice and skills is crucial if we, as practitioners, are to continue to provide the best support possible – for ourselves, our peers and the people we consult with. In our work we constantly bear witness to our clients' stories of hope, their dreams and acts of resistance to experiences that have been incredibly challenging.

88 *Dale moving out into the world*

> I encourage you to be innovative in your work with the people you see, holding value to their stories of preferred ways of being.

★★

What gives us hope in our work? My hope is that my walk with Dale, and many others who have been included in this book, *Reclaiming lives from sexual violence*, demonstrates the honouring of the people I see, above the problem story. I am hoping it is evident there is a mutual contribution in the therapeutic environment to a person's favoured stories of their lives and to what has been made possible through exploring experiences with the person. My hope is that I am no longer seen as the expert.

Through the use of narrative metaphors, Dale and others I have had the privilege of consulting with have gained a deeper understanding of shame while reclaiming their lives. Dale is now having the opportunity to contribute to others who have also experienced sexual violence, depriving the person that carried out the sexual violence in having the last say on matters of his identity (White 2005).

★★

> I am hoping that what you have witnessed with Dale and me encourages you to become curious in your own work, enabling you to think beyond the four walls of the clinical setting.

★★

14 Connecting it all together – linking neurobiology, the body and narrative practice with Dale's emotions, through story telling

Key points to consider

- The advancement in neuroplasticity: *The ability of neural networks in the brain to change through growth and reorganisation.*
- The client being able to name experiences in their own precise words and terms: *The client relating to the experiences regarding the changes in the body, attributed through their own understandings.*
- To not split emotion from meaning: *Keeping emotion/meaning/action together in your practice.*
  - *Interpreting someone's emotions in ways that are removed from your cultural prejudices.*

Trauma therapy is a rapidly growing field and current progresses in neuroscience have offered great insight into useful ways of working with the somatic impacts of trauma. Though what Dale and I offer is rather cognitive and emotionally focused, which aligns with narrative approaches, there is value in considering the mind and body effects when using narrative therapy. Narrative therapy deals with emotion in a particular way, connecting emotion and meaning, and refusing to separate them. Narrative therapy also refuses to separate emotion and meaning from action. The brain creates certain actions and sets the stage, but it doesn't necessarily make a person's experiences clear. Through social practices, concerning feelings and emotions and sensations, represented through the stories we tell, meaning and understanding is gained (Denborough 2019). Too often these stories are held private. Hence, it is about making meaning in relation to our body, and in this way people are able to put words and language to those experiences, and the person can have a relationship with those experiences. Then it is possible to introduce other modalities, for instance, EMDR, mindfulness (Carey et al. 2016).

Maggie Carey (2015) illustrates the concept that neurons that wire together fire together – as referenced from Donald Hebb, an influential psychologist in the 1940s – when speaking about the value of narrative therapy in stimulating rich story development focused on exceptions to a person's problem stories, thus creating a new narrative in the brain. Furthermore, the story metaphor enables a coordination of themes to emerge. Thus, meaning is able to be given to these lived experiences that shape our identity, bringing forth the inner experiences and making visible what the person gives value to.

DOI: 10.4324/9781003256816-15

90 *Connecting it all together*

The prospect of connection with our brain through experiences is traversable. In particular, the neural pathways for negative affect are already sizeable and smoothly paved, with many connections already established. Due to this, our problem stories in our lives are able to send the messages across our brain really quickly compared to what we may consider ordinary everyday experiences that are not as important in a person's memory. Over time, as our brains evolved, it was much more important that we responded to negative affect, and that we responded to fear and danger in our lives. Hence, we now have very quick pathways for responding to fight, flight, and freeze responses, such that we don't even have to think about it. Therefore, we are wired and set up to respond quickly to danger, and something that is fearful. Through negative affect these neuropathways are experienced. If you think of yourself as the problem, then you may experience a feeling of anxiety, a heaviness, attributed to the cortisol released in the brain, which is triggering the neural transmitters, particularly when you are experiencing something traumatic, such as sexual abuse. As a consequence, you may believe yourself to be useless, worthless and shameful. This belief becomes the person's default position, the problem stories get a hold, and the idea of these problem stories gets repeated and repeated until they become a (physical) superhighway of thought that claims our being, our thoughts about ourselves (Carey 2015).

Yet, what we have to our advantage is advancement of neuroplasticity, which is the ability of neural networks in the brain to change through growth and reorganisation. These changes range from individual neuron pathways making new connections to systematic adjustments like cortical remapping (Wittenberg 2009). Neuroplasticity was once thought by neuroscientists to manifest only during childhood, but research in the latter half of the 20th century showed that many aspects of the brain can be altered even through adulthood. Recent research confirms that neuroplasticity is possible when we have physical damage to the brain, where the brain is able to rewire itself (Shaffer 2016). Therefore, it is always possible to develop new pathways in the brain; it is always possible to develop new stories. Hence, with Dale we were able to explore his acts of resistance to the abuse, times he had physically resisted the abuser, times where he had spoken up against dominant masculinities and people's judgement – for instance, when Dale chose to grow his hair long – and together, we were able to deconstruct what this action represented for him. There is always a story behind the actions we take; our exploration of these stories commenced a positive stimulation of, or firing of, the neurotransmitters in Dale's brain that didn't pay attention to the problem stories. In narrative therapy, loitering around these taken-for-granted events commences the pathway to a person's rich story development. In narrative therapy, it is important in the scaffolding conversations to describe more about the events in a person's life, the physical context of actions taken, and exploring who wouldn't be surprised to hear the person taking action in this way. These lines of enquiry into a person's experiences add to the brain's development of positive emotions. Through exploring these emotions built up over time, we are actually bringing neurons together into these events of possibility, of actions taken that contradict the problem stories of the person's life. Through thickening up these stories so they are not just individual fragments, these neurons are built upon and wired together, creating a new single

Connecting it all together   91

pathway in the brain. Next time any of that memory is accessed, all of these positive emotions will come back. Furthermore, in narrative therapy, it is then possible to ask questions about the intentionality behind the actions taken, what the person is hoping, and what is important to them. Thus, during this questioning, a super-highway of positive emotion is being created through the firing of lots and lots of neurons (Carey 2015).

Through Dale being able to name his experience in his own precise words and terms (within externalising conversations), Dale was able to relate to the experiences regarding the changes in the body, attributed through his own understandings, as articulated below. My aim was not to conceal the consideration of politics (whether that related to gender, race, class, poverty, sexuality or other relations of power), which can be seen throughout the book, particularly when we were able to interview Dale's shame and then his integrity. In my own practice, my familiarity with neuroscience is quite limited, especially when combined with social sciences such as narrative therapy (Denborough 2019). Narrative therapy is interested in the real effects of how 'emotions' are understood and practised in particular times, places and cultures. Dale was able to reflect on ideas presented in narrative therapy and the effects on his mind and body and not separate himself from his past experiences (Denborough 2019).

> As a survivor of violent sexual abuse I needed to face the truth, the truth of my story, which I had locked away. I did not want to be separated from those emotions or evade them by a new coherent narrative that led more to the present. I wanted … (after pushing it deeply into my being for forty-two years) … to now dwell in and face the truth of my story of violent sexual abuse – by no longer denying the truth or being pushed to try and be separated from the truth, which was no longer denied. I wanted to understand it, therefore delving into the past was crucial to our work together. By unlocking the past history of my truths, a deeper understanding of shame was gained. Shame is one of those negative powerful emotions that controls – but naming it really does tame it slightly, when you understand how shame works. Dominant masculinity plays into shame, and I was able to understand this – and the effects – by interviewing shame, thus separating it from me. You can then approach it with that understanding – which in turn allowed me to push through shame's power. Understanding the way shame worked allowed me to see and handle the truths (as painful and excruciating as this was) and going through those painful truths supported me in seeing my innocence. Also, understanding the way I protected myself (learnt through being hurt more) made it more visible that I wasn't weak or pathetic. I needed to face the truth and not be separated from the past. Until you know the whole truth, I don't think you can ever be a whole person again, not until you know everything.
>
> Recently, when listening to an episode of *Insight* on the ABC, it was interesting to hear that people who had experienced sexual abuse struggled to get on with their lives or survive because there were parts of their memories missing. Therefore, to know our past in detail, we need to face it and understand it, so we can begin to deal with it and know more about who we are. Once I

92 *Connecting it all together*

came to the point of knowing and understanding my past fully and the true effects on my being – body, brain, sexuality, emotions – then I believe naming the truths of my experiences of sexual violence has stimulated the release of soothing neurotransmitters, thus modulating the fight, flight, freeze response resulting in positive emotions and giving a sense of relief, an opening space for a pivotal experience. Furthermore, I was able to name these effects and experience soothing sensations through narrative therapy, with externalising and scaffolding conversations, enabling me to name my experiences in my own words (which was always encouraged during therapy). The naming of my experiences in my own words drew me closer to the experiences, allowing me to fully experience the emotions and deconstruct what that meant for me. The practice of externalising, with scaffolding conversations, enabled me to name my truths, thus releasing the soothing neurotransmitters, which then enabled me to delve even more deeply into my truths and those things I had locked away because they were too shameful – truths I needed to understand – and the conversations with Tim allowed me to accept the truth of my story and work through the emotions experienced in my body with a deeper understanding of its history.

Furthermore, a consideration within my practice is to not split emotion from meaning, which is hazardous, as we can potentially engage in psychological colonisation without realising it, thinking that we can interpret someone's emotions in ways that are removed from our cultural prejudices (Denborough 2019). To highlight what this may look like in practice, I will use an example of effects Dale expressed in our first session, after writing his Victim Impact Statement after being told he had to appear in court regarding his past experiences of sexual abuse, as part of the Royal Commission (refer to page 31, in a transcript with Dale). Dale named that he had been '*crying a lot*' since his court appearance. Thus, emphasising this idea of keeping emotion / meaning / action together, I may do the following:

- Ask Dale what value is being expressed through those tears (linked to the concept of the absent but implicit, see White 2000)
- Honour the possible significance of Dale taking the step of sharing those tears and sorrows with me.
- Ask variations of the question, for instance: 'If those tears could speak, what might they say?'

In conclusion, when referring to Dale's emotions, David Denborough (2019) – referencing Michael White (2002) – emphasises that it is not thinking about the role of emotions but giving thought to how all expressions are expressions of experience, units of feeling, units of meaning, units of action, not separated up into one or the other. Thus with Dale, when he was expressing powerful emotions in our conversations, I was interested in those expressions and where they were taking him – where he might not otherwise have gotten to if he hadn't been expressing those emotions (Denborough 2019).

If you are interested in exploring the principles of neurobiology informing narrative therapy, here are two articles you can look into for yourself:

Zimmerman JL, Beaudoin MN (in press). Neurobiology for your narrative: How brain science can influence narrative work. *Journal of Systemic Therapies.*

Beaudoin MN, Zimmerman JL (2011). Narrative therapy and interpersonal neurobiology: revisiting classic practices, developing new emphases. *Journal of Systemic Therapies.* 30(1).

References

Anderson, Harlene and Goolishian, Harold (2007) 'The client is the expert: a not-knowing approach to therapy', *Therapy as a Social Construction*, SAGE Publications, Thousand Oaks, CA.

Carey, Maggie and Russell, Shona (2002) 'Re-membering: some answers to commonly asked questions', *International Journal of Narrative Therapy and Community Work*, 2, Dulwich Centre. Adelaide.

Carey, Maggie and Russell, Shona (2003) 'Re-authoring: some answers to commonly asked questions', *International Journal of Narrative Therapy and Community Work*, 3:60–71, Dulwich Centre, Adelaide.

Carey, Maggie, Walther, Sarah and Russell, Shona (2009) 'The absent but implicit: a map to support therapeutic enquiry', *Family Process*, 48:3, Research Library.

Carey, Maggie (2015) 'Gleanings from neuroscience', *Re-authoring teaching*. Retrieved from www.reauthoringteaching.com.

Carey, Maggie, Rosen, Lynne and Hamkins, SuEllen (2016) 'Bridging neurobiology, the body and narrative practice', *Re-authoring teaching*. Retrieved from www.reauthoring-teaching.com.

Clarke, Mary Ryllis (2018) *A Tear in the Glass*. Anchor Books, Australia.

Danaher, Shirato and Webb (2000) *Understanding Foucault*, Allen & Unwin, Australia.

Davidson, Sue (2015) Personal communication – Clinical supervision session.

Deborah, Cohen (2013) *Shames History*. Chicago Humanities Festival, www.chicagohumanities.org/events/2013/animal/shames-history.

Denborough, David (1996) 'Talking about men's violence, talking about prisons', *Beyond the Prison: Gathering Dreams of Freedom*, chapter 20, Dulwich Centre Publications, Adelaide.

Denborough, David (2008) *Collective Narrative Practice: Responding To Individuals, Groups, And Communities Who Have Experienced Trauma*, Dulwich Centre Publications, Adelaide.

Denborough, David (2015) Personal communication – Masters of narrative therapy assignment feedback.

Denborough, David (2019) 'Traveling down the neuro pathway, narrative practice, neuroscience, bodies, emotions and the effective turn', *International Journal of Narrative Therapy and Community Work*, (3): 13–53, Dulwich Centre. Adelaide.

Epston, David and White, Michael (1990) 'Consulting your consultants: the documentation of alternative knowledges', *Dulwich Centre Newsletter*, 4:25–35. Republished 1992 in Epston and White: *Experience, contradiction, narrative & imagination: selected papers of David Epston & Michael White, 1989–1991*, chapter 1, pp. 11–26.

Erskine, Richard (1997) *Theories and Methods of an Integrative Transactional Analysis. A Volume of Selected Articles*, TA Press, USA.

References   95

Findlay, Ron (2013) adapted from the work of White, Michael (2005) *Michael White workshop notes*, September 21 2005, www.dulwichcentre.com.au/michael-white-workshop-notes.pdf, Dulwich Centre, Adelaide.

Foucault, Michel (1995) *Discipline and Punish: The Birth of the Prison*, 1st edition (1 October 1989), KNOPF, New York, NY.

Frayling, Maureen (2010) 'Spreading the news: therapeutic letters in the health care setting', A review of a special edition of the *Journal of Family Nursing*, 15:1, Dulwich Centre, Adelaide.

Handsacker, Renee (2012) 'Opening up of the counselling room – the joining of stories as a political act', *International Journal of Narrative Therapy and Community Work*, 3:1–10.

Hayward, Clarissa (2006) *On Power and Responsibility*, Published by the Political Studies Association and Blackwell Publishing.

Jenkins, Alan (1993) *Invitations to Responsibility. The Therapeutic Engagement of Men who are Violent and Abusive*, Dulwich Centre Publications, Adelaide.

Jenkins, Alan (1998) 'Invitations to responsibility', in Marshall, Fernandez, Hudson, Ward (eds) *Sourcebook of Treatment Programs for Sexual Offenders* (pp. 163–189). Applied Clinical Psychology. Springer, Boston, MA.

Jenkins, Alan (2007) 'Discovering integrity: working with shame without shaming young people who have sexually abused', *Current Perspectives – Working with Sexually Aggressive Youth and Youth with Sexual Behaviour Problems*, chapter 17, NEARI Press. USA.

Jenkins, Alan (2009) 'Attending to ethical possibilities', *Becoming Ethical. A Parallel, Political Journey with Men Who Have Abused*, chapter 4, Russell House Publishing, United Kingdom.

McLean, Christopher, Carey, Maggie, White, Cheryl (1996) *Men's Ways of Being*. Taylor and Francis Group LLC (Books), New York, NY.

Nelson, Hilde Lindemann (2001). *Damaged Identities, Narrative Repair*. Cornell University Press, Ithaca, NY.

Lewis, Michael (1992) *Shame: The Exposed Self*, Free Press, New York, NY.

Lewis, Helen B (1971) *Shame and Guilt in Neurosis*, International University Press, New York, NY.

Mann, Sue and Russell, Shona (2002) 'Narrative ways of working with women survivors of childhood sexual violence', *International Journal of Narrative Therapy and Community Work*, 2002(3): 3–22. Dulwich Centre, Adelaide.

Morgan, Alice and White, Michael (2006) *Narrative Therapy with Children and Their Families*, Dulwich Centre Publications, Adelaide.

Morgan, Alice (2000) *What is Narrative Therapy? An Easy-to-Read Introduction*, Dulwich Centre Publications, Adelaide.

Rayyan, Nihaya Mahmud Abu (2009) 'Seasons of life: ex-detainees reclaiming their lives', *International Journal of Narrative Therapy and Community Work*, 2009(2): 24–40, Dulwich Centre, Adelaide.

Shaffer, Joyce (2016). 'neuroplasticity and clinical practice: building brain power for health', *Frontiers in Psychology*, 7: 1118. doi:10.3389/fpsyg.2016.01118. PMC 4960264. PMID 27507957.

SNAICC (2014) *Caring for kids – What is pride? – What is meant by shame in Aboriginal cultures?* http://www.supportingcarers.snaicc.org.au/caring-for-kids/pride/

White, Michael (1995) *Re-authoring Lives: Interviews and Essays*, Dulwich Centre Publications. Adelaide.

White, Michael (2000) *Reflections on Narrative Practice – Essays and Interviews*, Dulwich Centre Publications, Adelaide.

White, M. (2000a). 'Re-engaging with history: the absent but implicit', in M. White (ed) *Reflections on Narrative Practice: Essays and Interviews* (pp. 35–58). Dulwich Centre Publications, Adelaide.

96 References

White, Michael (2001) 'Narrative practice and the unpacking of identity conclusions', *Gecko: A Journal of Deconstruction and Narrative Ideas in Therapeutic Practice*, 1:28–55. Dulwich Centre Publications, Adelaide.

White, M. (2002a, August 6). Untitled [Video recording]. *Michael White Video Archive (Tape 192)*. Dulwich Centre, Adelaide.

White, Michael (2002b) 'Journey metaphors', *International Journal of Narrative Therapy and Community Work*, 2002(4): 12–18. Dulwich Centre, Adelaide.

White, Michael (2003) 'Narrative practice and community assignments', *International Journal of Narrative Therapy and Community Work*, 2:17–56. Referenced from Jill Freedmann (2012) 'Explorations of the absent but implicit', *International Journal of Narrative Therapy and Community Work*, 4: 1–10, Dulwich Centre, Adelaide.

White, Michael (2004) *Folk psychology and narrative practice*, 21 September 2005, Folk psychology and narrative practice (dulwichcentre.com.au). Dulwich Centre, Adelaide.

White, Michael (2005) *Michael White workshop notes*, 21 September 2005, www.dulwichcentre.com.au/michael-white-workshop-notes.pdf, Dulwich Centre, Adelaide.

White, Michael (2007a) *Maps of Narrative Practice*. Norton Professional Books, New York, NY.

White, Michael (2007b) *Trauma and Narrative Therapy. Part 1*, dulwichcentre.com.au/michael-white-archive/michael-white-video-archive, International Trauma Studies Program, New York.

White, Michael (2011) 'Turning points and the significance of personal and community ethics', in M. White (ed) *Narrative Practice: Continuing the Conversations* (pp. 27–44). Norton, New York, NY. Referenced from Kelsi Semeschuk (2019) 'Refusing to separate critique from respect', *International Journal of Narrative Therapy and Community Work*, 3:9, Dulwich Centre, Adelaide.

Wittenberg F. George (2009) 'Experience, cortical remapping, and recovery in brain disease'. Published online 2009 Sep 19. doi: 10.1016/j.nbd.2009.09.007. Retrieved from Experience, Cortical Remapping, and Recovery in Brain Disease (nih.gov).

Yuen, Angel (2007) 'Discovering children's responses to trauma: a response-based narrative practice', *International Journal of Narrative Therapy and Community Work*, 2007:3, Dulwich Centre. Adelaide.

Winslade, John (2005) 'Utilising discursive positioning in counselling', *British Journal of Guidance and Counselling*, 33: 351–364, 3 August 2005.

Wingard, Barbara (2011) 'Bringing lost ones into our conversation', *International Journal of Narrative Therapy and Community Work*, 1:54–56, Dulwich Centre, Adelaide.

Appendix A

Therapeutic letter
Responding to trauma

Mathew's action of life/bravery

When there were terrible things happening Mathew was scared, Mathew would pretend to get out of it by crying (fakely) and Mathew would be very angry at everyone for no reason at all. Mathew would stay close to his Mum and Dad and think positively like it will be just fine, I won't see him again he will go to prison. Mathew had lots of thoughts like to snuggle with Tina (his cat) because Tina is close and there to keep him safe. If somebody was to look at Mathew back in them days, they would probably think 'Mathew's acting differently than usual' after all that has happened, they probably now say 'look Mathew is back he is finally his wild self!' once again!!!!

Appendix B

Narrative Maps

| **Externalising conversations includes the statement of position maps**
 <u>Statement of position maps method (White 2005):</u>
 - Naming the problem / unique outcome using the words of the person
 - Naming the effects of the problem / unique outcome using the person's words
 - Evaluating the effects of the problem / unique outcome using the person's words, i.e. good / bad / both
 - Naming the person's values and main beliefs stemming from the evaluation of the effects of the problem / unique outcome | Focuses on problems that may once have been internalised and totalising of the person. Externalises the problem in a non-judging way of looking at the problem. Once problems are externalised and not viewed as if they don't simply exist as an innate aspect of a person they can then be put into storylines. It is now possible to ask questions about how long the depression has been an influence in someone's life, when it came into their life, if there were factors that contributed to its entry, what the real effects of the depression are (on the person, their relationships and others). These sorts of questions begin to place the existence of the problem into a storyline. Broader considerations can now be taken into account when it is understood that people's relationships with problems are shaped by history and culture and their values and beliefs. It is possible to explore how gender, race, culture, sexuality, class and other relations of power have influenced the construction of the problem (www.dulwichcentre.gor.gau/ externalising). |

(Continued)

Appendix B

Re-authoring conversations Re-authoring map method (White 2005): past history, present, future - Landscape of consciousness (identity) - Intentional understandings of self - Understandings about what is given value to - Internal understandings of self - Realisations about self - Learning's to take away - Landscape of action - Events in your life - Circumstances in your life - Sequence of events - Time of the events - Plot / Story of the events	Involves the identification and co-creation of alternative storylines of identity. The practice of re-authoring is based on the assumption that no one story can possibly sum up the entirety of a person's experience; there will always be inconsistencies and contradictions. There will always be other storylines that can be created from the events of our lives. As such, our identities are not single-storied – no one story can sum us up. We are multi-storied. Re-authoring conversations involve the co-authoring of storylines that will assist in addressing whatever predicaments have brought someone into counselling. What sort of storyline an event is placed into makes a significant difference as to the effects of that event in a person's life. These storylines are shaped by many influences, relationships, events and broader relations of power (Carey and Russell 2003).
Re-membering conversations Re-membering map method (White 2005): - Contribution of a significant person to the figure's identity, i.e. their values and beliefs - Contribution of a significant person to the figure's life, i.e. experiences - Contribution of the person to the significant figure's identity, i.e. their values and beliefs - Contribution of the person to the significant figure's life, i.e. experiences	Calling attention to the significant figures that belong to one's life story. People's identities are shaped by what can be referred to as a 'club of life'. This 'club of life' metaphor introduces the idea that for all of us there are members to our club of life who have had particular parts to play in how we have come to experience ourselves. The person stands with significant others in this preferred territory of their identity, and these connections provide a great deal of support for the preferred actions they may wish to take (Carey and Russell 2002).

Appendix C

Interview with 'Shame' practice questions

Please think of a situation where you have experienced shame. In pairs, take turns to ask the following questions.

Practitioner:
Before we interview you, playing the role of Shame, is it okay to gain an understanding of what shame means to you?

Consultant:

Practitioner:
How would you define or explain shame to me, to others? [You may have used other words, pictures and images that are more useful to you].

Consultant:

Practitioner:
What is the value of making this meaning?

Consultant:

Practitioner:
Are you okay if we now interview Shame? It may feel a little strange and if it gets too difficult just let me know. Are you okay to give it a go and see how it goes, Shame?

Consultant:

Practitioner:
Tell me about yourself and how you have worked in [consultant's name]'s life.

Consultant:

Practitioner:
When did you first come into [consultant's name]'s life?

Appendix C

Consultant:

Practitioner:
What do you think [consultant's name] remembers about their life before you came along?

Consultant:

Practitioner:
What tactics do you or did you use to trick [consultant's name]?

Consultant:

Practitioner:
What do you help others to believe about [consultant's name]?

Consultant:

Practitioner:
How much of [consultant's name]'s life do you or have you taken up?

Consultant:

Practitioner:
Who else stands behind you to help you?

Consultant:

Practitioner:
Do you have any allies that you rely on for extra assistance?

Consultant:

Practitioner:
What lies have you been telling (past, present, in the future)?

Consultant:

Practitioner:
How useful are you to [consultant's name]?

Consultant:

Practitioner:
What does being in [consultant's name]'s life say about shame?

102   *Appendix C*

Consultant:

Practitioner:
What beliefs do you inspire in [consultant's name]?

Consultant:

Practitioner:
What plans have you influenced [consultant's name] to make?

Consultant:

Practitioner:
What purpose do you serve in [consultant's name]'s life?

Consultant:

Practitioner:
Can you remember a time when you left [consultant's name] to get on with their life?

Consultant:

Practitioner:
What would life be like without you?

Consultant:

Practitioner:
What would [consultant's name] like to ask you, if they were in the room?

Consultant:

Practitioner:
When you think about your influence over [consultant's name], how have other social contexts influenced how you work? Let me see – like the role of their gender, i.e. being (female, male, non-binary). Does this make sense, Shame?

Consultant:

Practitioner:
What does Shame say about what it is to be a (female, male, non-binary) in today's world?

Consultant:

Practitioner:

Appendix C 103

Is Shame aware of any other dominating thoughts that keep them alive in [consultant's name]'s life?

Consultant:

Practitioner:
What will you take away from this interview? Are there particular words of resonance that you haven't shared before, a learning, an image?

Consultant:
#Additional questions for consideration that you may wish to explore in your own practice setting when interviewing Shame or any named problem story could be:

- What lessens the effects that shame has?
- What are the other influences on [consultant's name]'s life that has them taking steps towards their preferred practices of living?
- Who are the allies in this moving away from Shame's influences . . . ?
- What does shame suggest to [consultant's name] about what is important to them?

Appendix D

Interview with 'Integrity' practice questions

Please think of a situation where you have silenced Shame (even if a little) and spoken up – made a stand for what you believe in. In pairs, take turns to ask the following questions.

Practitioner:
Before we interview you, playing the role of Integrity, is it okay to gain an understanding of what integrity means to you?

Consultant:

Practitioner:
How would you define or explain integrity to me, to others? [You may have used other words, pictures and images that are more useful to you].

Consultant:

Practitioner:
What is the value of making this meaning?

Consultant:

Practitioner:
Okay, let's now attempt to interview you as Integrity; let me know if this becomes too confusing or isn't working.

Consultant:

Practitioner:
If 'Integrity' had a gender and a colour what would they be?

Consultant:

Practitioner:
Knowing what you now know about yourself, Integrity, is there anything you would like to ask Shame if they were in the room?

Appendix D   105

Consultant:

Practitioner:
Is this positive / negative? Somewhere in between, a bit of both?

Consultant:

Practitioner:
So, when we think about the power practices of Shame, are you surprised about what you have shared, now and when looking back?

Consultant:

Practitioner:
When Integrity first started to come and see [practitioner's name] for counselling, would you have been surprised to hear them talk about Shame in this way?

Consultant:

Practitioner:
Do you have any other allies?

Consultant:

Practitioner:
When did you first become aware of what it means to be [female, male, non-binary] in your own life? I.e. was there anything that you were taught as a child ... remember seeing in the school yard . . . watching on TV?

Consultant:

Practitioner:
What is your view of Shame now?

Consultant:

Practitioner:
So, when we look at what [consultant's name] values in their life and their belief systems – has this changed throughout the time we have spent 'walking alongside' each other?

Consultant:

Practitioner:
Is it stronger or weaker now – your sense of who you are, or rather, who you have always been?

106 *Appendix D*

Consultant:

Practitioner:
What would you call it, i.e. naming who you are?

Consultant:

Practitioner:
Who wouldn't be surprised to hear you talk about yourself in this way?

Consultant:

Practitioner:
When did they first know this about you?

Consultant:

Practitioner:
How is this affecting you now?

Consultant:

Practitioner:
Who have you recruited along the way regarding your values and beliefs? Who has always been there that wouldn't be surprised to hear you talk about yourself in this way?

Consultant:

Practitioner:
So, what defines you now?

Consultant:

Practitioner:
Is there anything you would like to say to [consultant's name] if they were in the room now?

Consultant:

Practitioner:
Is there anything that you will take away from this discussion about Integrity in our conversation? E.g. words said, a thought, an image.

Appendix D

Consultant:

Practitioner:
How will this be used in a practical way?

Consultant:

Practitioner:
If you were [consultant's name]'s child how would you be impacted by what she has shared and who she is as a person?

Consultant:

Practitioner:
That makes me a little curious. Has this got anything to do with what [consultant's name] now believes is true about theirself? Or have you reclaimed what you already knew about yourself, if that makes sense?

Consultant:

Practitioner:
Was there anything that was useful about today?

Consultant:

Appendix E

Re-membering Conversations practice map questions

Please think of a person who would not be surprised that you are doing the kinds of work that you do. In pairs, take turns to ask the following categories of enquiry.

1. Topic: What this person contributed to your life …
    - Tell me something about this person – how did you come to know each other?
    - Did you share particular activities or ideas?
    - What did this person bring to your life?
    - What difference has knowing this person made to your life?
    - Did you learn something from this person?
    - How have these influences affected your life?

2. Topic: Your identity through this person's life …
    - In light of what you have been describing, what do you think this person saw in you?
    - What did they know about you?
    - What do you think they appreciated about you?
    - What difference did it make to you that you were seen in this way?
    - If this person was here right now, what might they want to tell me about you?

3. Topic: What you might have contributed to this person's life …
    - Can you imagine what it might have been like for this person to know you?
    - What do you think it meant to them to have you in their life?
    - Do you think there may have been some way that you contributed to their life?

4. Topic: Your contribution to the person's identity …

    - Do you think you contributed to this person's sense of who they were or what they stood for?
    - Was anything made possible for this person through knowing you?

Appendix E 109

- If this person was here and able to hear about their importance to you, what would this be like for you?
- How do you think this person's life was different for knowing you in the way they did?
- What might this person say about the ways in which you contributed to their life, to who they were as a person, to what their life was about?

This version by a colleague, Ron Findlay (2013) adapted from the work of Michael White (2005).

Appendix F

Tree of life project

PROJECT OVERVIEW

This approach enables people to speak about their lives in ways that make them stronger. It involves people drawing their own 'tree of life' in which they get to speak of their 'roots' (where they come from), their skills and knowledges, their hopes and dreams, as well as the special people in their lives. The participants then join their trees into a 'forest of life' and, in groups, discuss some of the 'storms' that affect their lives and ways that they respond to these storms, protect themselves and each other.

The Roots (textual heritage, i.e. past history of experiences) The roots of the tree are a prompt for you to think about and write on your tree where you come from (village, town, country), your family history (origins, family name, ancestry, extended family), names of people who have taught you the most in life, your favourite place at home, a treasured song or dance.

The Ground (your present landscape of action, i.e. what are you doing now) The ground is the place for you to write where you live now and activities you are engaged with in your daily life. The ground represents where you live at present, and some of the activities that you choose to do each day. Include some of the things that you are doing or learning.

The Trunk (what is valued / skills) The trunk of the tree is an opportunity for you to write your skills and abilities (i.e. skills of caring, loving and kindness) and what you are good at.

The Branches (horizons) The branches of the tree are where you write your hopes, dreams and wishes for the directions of your life.

The Leaves (Re-membering lives) The leaves of the tree represent significant people in your life, who may be alive or may have passed on – i.e.

Appendix F 111

> how have/had they contributed to your life, your sense of self ... how have/ had you contributed to their life, sense of self.
>
> **The Fruits** The fruits of the tree represent gifts you have been given – not necessarily material gifts; gifts of being cared for, of being loved, acts of kindness.
>
> **The Flowers / Seeds (legacies we wish to leave)** The flowers of the tree represent thoughts, actions, contributions you wish to leave for people, changes you want to make to/for others who have experienced oppression, been marginalised – i.e. tips to reveal you're no longer being silenced. For example, how would you like to contribute to others, in a meaningful way, knowing what you now know about your own experiences of shame?
>
> **The Compost Heap** Write down anything in your compost heap that would normally go in the other sections described above but which are now things you no longer want to be defined by. You can write down places, people, problems, experiences. Whatever you need to.

This version by Tim Donovan (2017) adapted from the work of David Denborough (2008)

Tree of life questions

The roots (textual heritage, i.e. past history of experiences):

When thinking about the roots and what that evokes – e.g. difficult things/injustices/abuse – it's worth including not only the hardship (on the left) ... then on the other side of the same root, write what resonates in relation to whatever learning/ determination/response you have made in relation to this (on the right).

- What's your history of making a stand for what's right, and who taught you that?
- What's your history of looking after yourself? What skills have you used in the past?
- Have there been any past experiences that have taught you how to better look after yourself now? How can you remind yourself of these abilities you have when you experience tough times – at work, at home, with family?
- Is there anyone that has contributed to your life, .e.g. who showed you how to care for others and inspired you to make a difference?
- What did you learn from them?
- Would they be surprised to hear that you have mentioned them in this way?
- Is there a book that reminds you of what is important to you?
- Do you have a favourite song, movie that reminds you of what is important to you, e.g. showing compassion, standing up for what you believe?
- Is there a favourite place that you go to / visit that gives you solace – i.e. connects you to what you value?
- What are your intentions of going to this place?
- Is there something that connects you to your history of learning – e.g. a person, a place, a book?

112 *Appendix F*

The ground (your present landscape of action, i.e. what are you doing now):

- Who grounds you now in being aware of your compassion for others, wanting to make a difference in people's lives?
- Who grounds you now in being aware of times when work or home life, is getting in the way of you living your life in your preferred way?
- What reminds you now of the importance you place on caring for others, making a difference?
- What do you do currently to stand up for what's right and positively affect others?
- What experiences currently exist that silence you from speaking up for what's right?
- Have there been examples of how you have or haven't been able to speak up in uncovering the truth behind someone's experiences – i.e. challenging judgement from others or towards others? What did you learn from this?

The trunk (what is valued/skills)

- What are your hopes for the people you consult with and the people you work alongside in your work?
- What motivates you in the work that you do?
- What skills have you learnt from speaking up for people who have experienced oppression in their lives, speaking up for family members?
- What is being made possible from what you now know about what motivates you in your work?
- What have some of the positive effects of knowing right from wrong been in your life?

The branches (horizons)

- What contributions – regarding speaking up for people experiencing oppression, being marginalised and not being treated fairly – have you seen and are now talking about for the future?
- What have you learnt from this?
- What steps will you take to make this happen? What are your intentions behind this?
- Who wouldn't be surprised to hear that you are interested in this way of thinking?
- What is now possible for you from this way of thinking?

The leaves of the tree (re-membering lives)

- Has there been anyone that has reminded you of the importance of speaking up for what's right, showing compassion, sharing the truth? Has there been anyone that reminds you about the value of looking after yourself in the work that you do?
- How have they contributed to your understanding of what's right, social justice, fairness etc?

Appendix F 113

- How have you contributed to their life? What would they want to say, if they were in the room today?
- What have you learnt from these/this person(s)?
- Has anyone inspired you, been 'walking alongside' you, to give you support when standing up for what's right, showing compassion?
- Would they be surprised that you have included them?
- How have you contributed to others in a positive way when standing up for what's right, or showing compassion, that has reflected your own history of learning – e.g. to your children, friends, family, pets?

Fruits (legacies bequeathed of us)

- What have you been able to take away with you that acknowledges this journey with standing up for what's right, showing compassion, in a positive way? What motivates you during the tough times? What gives you hope?
- Is this surprising to hear?
- What have you learnt about your values and beliefs along the way to being interested in this way of thinking?

Flowers/Seeds (legacies we wish to leave)

- What contributions are you currently making to others in standing up for the truth and caring for others?
- How can you contribute to other people, colleagues and friends that invigorates you to remain in this profession?
- How can you speak up for people who are experiencing oppression etc.?
- How can your individual story be honoured in a way that can now contribute to social action that challenges the dominant beliefs/assumptions surrounding people who experience oppression and/or who are marginalised?

If you are doing this practice as a group, you can put all the Tree of Life posters together – e.g. on a wall – and explore in the group the textual heritage of some of these skills of compassion and standing up for others, by asking:

- How did you learn/these strengths?
- Where did you learn them?

Compost heap

- What type of compost heap will you use and what is its significance – e.g. open air, enclosed etc.
- In the compost heap, write down anything that would normally go in the other sections of the tree but which are now things you no longer want to be defined by.
- Write down places, people, problems, and/or experiences, which can often be sources of trauma, abuse, cultural standards of normality/beauty/etc. or anything else that shapes negative thoughts about yourself in your mind.

114 *Appendix F*

- When you refer to what you have added to the compost heap, do these things stay and go back into the soil because they further add to your integrity?

The storms in your life

- What may get in the way of speaking your truths?
- What may prove challenging, when standing up for what's right?
- How can you use your strengths, skills, abilities, individually, and/or collectively with others, to overcome/stay strong against the storms in your life?

This version by Tim Donovan (2017) adapted from the work of David Denborough (2008)

Appendix G

Dale's Tree of Life

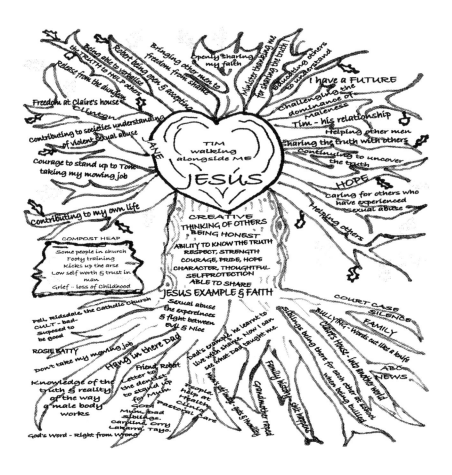

Figure G.1 Dale's adaptation of his Tree of Life.

Appendix H

Signs of social and psychological resistance

PART 1: DURING THE EXPERIENCES OF SEXUAL VIOLENCE
Tried to protect yourself during the experiences of sexual violence: physically and/or emotionally. What steps did you take? Some of them you may have already spoken about.
Displayed acts of caring, concern, comfort for others during the experiences of sexual violence: (may include caring for friends, children or other adults) that allowed you to stand up for what is right in your life. Tell me more about these experiences of knowing what was right?
Received comfort from others during the experiences of sexual violence (was able to take this in):
Displayed acts of caring for oneself during the experiences of sexual violence. How much courage does it take to think about these times? What things did you do to care for yourself during these times?
Displayed acts of dignity or pride during your experiences of sexual violence: not allowing for the effects of shame to have an influence.
Found ways to hold onto hope during the experiences of sexual violence: may include spiritual, faith practices: having power over the effects of shame

PART 2: AFTER THE EXPERIENCES OF SEXUAL VIOLENCE
Displaying acts of caring, concern, comfort for others after the experiences of sexual violence (may include friends, children or other adults).
Receiving comfort from others (is able to take this in): maximising the impacts of value for yourself and others. What do these acts say about what you value? What are your intentions for receiving comfort from others?
Taking steps to try to reclaim things of significance: being aware of the effects of your own values and beliefs and sharing the truth.
Making plans to rebuild parts of your life from what has been silenced / forgotten by your experiences of sexual violence: what are the effects of acknowledging your own values of knowing what's right and wrong making possible in your life?
Speaking with others or listening to others about their experiences of sexual violence in ways that contribute to feeling joined and stronger: minimising the effects of shame and strengthening your sharing of the truth.
Able to find joy in small moments within life, minimising the effects of shame, overpowering the effects of shame and allowing for the effects of sharing the truth and knowing right from wrong to be influenced.

Appendix H 117

| Linking with others through song, music, prayer, art and so on, to share experiences, sorrows, hopes and dreams: allowing for your values and beliefs to be influenced. |
| Finding ways to take action either individually or with others that are in accord with what hopes or dreams you have for your life: exploring the effects that your knowledge of sharing the truth and knowing what's right is having on future decisions. |

This version by Tim Donovan (2017) adapted from the work of David Denborough (2008).

Index

Pages in *italics* refer figures and **bold** refer tables.

accountability 10

Beaudoin, M. N. 93

Carey, Maggie 18, 89
child sexual violence: breaks the silence of 58; institutional responses to 86; memories of 30; survival of 40
Christian values 36, 42, 44
client(s): consulting respectfully with 10; conversation with 11; own experiences of sexual violence 34; personal experiences 11–12; positive identity conclusions 24; relationship with shame 31
Cohen, Deborah 13
compassion for people 26–27, 29
counselling 53, 56

Dale's experiences of sexual violence 1–2, 31; externalising conversation 15–16, 26, 35; friendship with Robert, after 64; interview with shame 38; judging people 50; resistance 25, 85; revealing control of the perpetrator *34*; by Ridsdale 72–74; shame *see* shame; signs of social and psychological resistance **82–85**; silencing of 18–19
Denborough, David 2, 52, 55–56, 62, 69–70, 81

externalising conversations 15–16, 35, 44; usefulness of 26

Findlay, Ron 109
'folk psychology,' 52
Foucault, Michel 16, 38, xv

Handsacker, Renee 75
Hebb, Donald 89
hegemonic masculinity 18, 34

Inglewood Catholic presbytery 42
integrity 11–12, 30–32, **32**, 40–41, 44
interview: 'integrity' practice questions 104–107; 'shame' practice questions 100–103

Jenkins, Alan 2, 11, 14, 30
Johns, Dale: ability 8, 45–46, 65; brain 90; capacity 33; compassion for people 26–27, 29; compost heap 68–69; confusion 37–38; counsellor Tim 56; 'crying a lot,' 92; dad carry himself after the sexual violence 46; dad's living memory 47; emotions 38, 92; experiences of sexual violence *see* Dale's experiences of sexual violence; faith in Jesus 40, 68; family's expectations 60; fault 36–37; fear 42; forgive himself 43; hard-won living skills 20; history of making a stand 63; honesty 22; ideas of self 29–30; innocence 21; integrity 30–32, **32**, 40–41, 44; journey with shame *see* shame; 'keep sharing' and 'making a stand,' 22–23; lived experiences where he is not alone *70*; long-held ideas 30; mum and dad 46–48, 63; new identity conclusions 45, 50, 79; own skills and knowledges 25–26; and Paul's knowledge 57; people of significance, sharing the truth **67**; positive identity conclusions 29; relationship between personal experiences of abuse 34; responding to an adult male in prison 56–57; rich story

Index 119

development 55; sense of guilt 36; sexuality 38; shit and the darkness 59–60; speak directly to Shame 50–52; 'stop the silence ... stop the sexual abuse,' 86; therapeutic journey 87–88; truths 50; unconditional love 44; value awareness 29, 31, 42; violently sexually abuse by Ridsdale 72–74

Lewis, Michael 13
long-held beliefs 24

male pain 18
masculinity 18–19
Mathew's action of life/bravery 97
McLean, Christopher 18
men's pain 18–19
Men's ways of being (1996) 18–19
metaphor 27–28; 'rites of passage,' 39–40
Morgan, Alice 62
myths 1, 3

narrative maps 98–99
narrative therapy 2, 55, 74; body effects 89–91; and interpersonal neurobiology 93; practice methods **3–6**
Ncube, Ncazelo 62
negative identity conclusions 20–21
Nelson, Hilde Lindemann 75
neuropathways for negative affect 90

positive identity conclusions 21

reclaiming integrity framework 31, **32**
relationships building: accountability 10; beliefs and assumptions of culture 11; developing attitude of reverence 11; open relationship 11; transparency 10; working collaboratively 11
re-membering conversations 26; map method 99; practice map questions 108–109
rich story development 25
Ridsdale, Gerald 25
Ridsdale's sexual violence 33, 42–45; local Catholic priest, Inglewood, Victoria 71; violently sexually abused story 72–74

'rites of passage' metaphor 39–40
Royal Commission 59–60, 86, 92

Secretariat of National Aboriginal and Islander Child Care (SNAICC) 13
sexual abuse: prevalence of 55; by Ridsdale 72–74
sexual violence: overruled 42; power practices of the person 23, 33
shame 14–15; as an externalised emotion 34; confusion around 60; deconstructing 35; deeper understanding of 29; definition 13; freedom from 58; influence in sexual abuse 55; influence of 1; and integrity 43; notion of 13; overcome the effects of 64–65; to piss off 41; uncovering truth of 67
Shame: the exposed self 13
'shared space,' 2
sharing stories 54; truth 56, 59; two males to share the truth 75, **76–78**
SNAICC *see* Secretariat of National Aboriginal and Islander Child Care
society's beliefs and assumptions 35
statement of position maps 21; method 98
stories to problem story 8

trauma 24; responding to 97; therapy 89
'Tree of Life' metaphor 62, 65–66, 69–70, 79

values and beliefs 29
vulnerability 9

'walking alongside,' 2, 18, 24, 30, 36, 49, 61, 75
White, Cheryl 18
White, M. xv, 2–3, 7–8, 10, 23, 31, 39, 52, 98–99, 109
Wingard, Barbara 13
Winslade, John 35, 38

Yuen, Angel 8

Zimmerman, J. L. 93

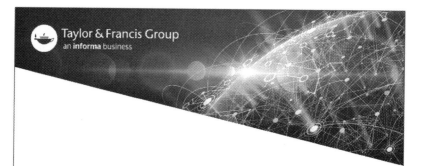

Printed in the United States
by Baker & Taylor Publisher Services